Writers of Wales

EDITORS

MEIC STEPHENS   R. BRINLEY JONES

GWYN THOMAS

Ian Michael

GWYN

THOMAS

University of Wales Press
on behalf of the Welsh Arts Council

1977

H31 217 8774

I

It is a rare event in literary history when the first three works of an author are all published in the space of a year. It is even rarer when their readers and critics are generally agreed that the works are the product of a man 'writing from strength' in a startlingly new and original style. This remarkable way of writing was exhibited in a collection of *novelle* and short stories, WHERE DID I PUT MY PITY?, and in two short novels, THE DARK PHILOSOPHERS and THE ALONE TO THE ALONE, which appeared between the summers of 1946 and 1947, when Gwyn Thomas was in his thirty-fourth year, but it had not come about overnight.

Born on 6th July 1913 in Cymmer, near Porth in the Rhondda Valley, Gwyn was the youngest of the twelve children of an unemployed miner. His mother died when he was still a small child, and his eldest sister Nana brought up the family. Educated at Porth Grammar School, he won a State Scholarship to Oxford to read Modern Languages in 1930. In 1933, with the aid of a Miners' Scholarship, he spent six months at the University of Madrid, during the exciting days of the short-lived Second Spanish Republic. After graduating in 1934, he worked for four years as W.E.A. lecturer associated with the Maesyrhâf settlement at Trealaw, and it was this period that created the novelist in him, as he himself has recounted:

I worked for years as W.E.A. lecturer up and down the Glamorgan valleys, the hardest and most vitalising phase, brought to complete fulfilment the attitude and expression for which I had been groping. I wrote a novel called SORROW FOR THY SONS *for a competition run by Gollancz who was looking for a novel on unemployment. It was based on the troubles of the anti-means test campaign in which I had served as committee-man and refulgent orator. The novel was praised but turned down by the firm's advisers who thought the bitterness of the work so wild and searing it would be read only by readers with asbestos underwear.*

(in ARTISTS IN WALES, *ed. Meic Stephens, p. 71)*

After his marriage to Lyn Thomas in 1938, he went to Manchester to work as area officer of the National Council of Social Service in South-East Lancashire and North-East Cheshire, but in 1940 he was appointed Spanish master at Cardigan Grammar School, transferring to Barry Grammar School in 1942. Before 1940 he had completed WHERE DID I PUT MY PITY?, and in that year he wrote THE DARK PHILOSOPHERS. Later, in Barry, he wrote THE ALONE TO THE ALONE. At the war's end, when paper rationing was partially relaxed, Mrs Thomas consulted THE WRITERS' AND ARTISTS' YEAR BOOK and, knowing nothing of publishers' options, sent off each of the three completed works to a different publisher. When all three were separately accepted, she had to call in a literary agent to sort out the resulting contractual confusion.

The delay in publication caused by the war meant that the author's style, by continual practice, had begun to mature before any of his books were launched. This is not to say that he was wont to polish or revise his stories and novels; his usual practice, in his schoolteaching days, was to take a short nap on returning home and then to write about 2,000 words in long hand in exercise books until about half past eight, when he would usually accompany his wife on a stroll. His wife typed all his manuscripts and later corrected the proofs. Only since his retirement from teaching to become a freelance writer and broadcaster in 1962 has his timetable been modified to the extent of his writing earlier in the day, in his peaceful house at Peterston-super-Ely.

The style which struck contemporary readers as so original and racy can be seen in its 'first state' in 'Oscar', the longest tale in WHERE DID I PUT MY PITY?:

Rainwater streamed down the walls of the 'Harp'. It had rained for a week. There was nothing of the many things I could feel around me in the dark that was not soaked. I wore a waterproof jacket. That jacket was thick and good. It had belonged to an uncle of mine. I took it from his house without telling anybody, just after he died. The rain did not bother him any more. It bothered me.

I leaned with the full weight of my shoulders against the walls of the 'Harp'. I was standing in the yard of that pub. The rain bounced down from the chutes about six inches from where I stood. Besides me was a lighted window, small. The light from that window was very yellow and had a taste.

Behind that window were about a dozen drunks, singing. Among those drunks was Oscar. I could tell that Oscar's voice if I was deaf. There was a feel about it, a slow greasy feel.

Oscar was a hog. I knew him well. I worked for Oscar. I was Oscar's boy. It was for Oscar I was waiting in that streaming, smelling yard of the 'Harp', pressing my shoulders against those walls that were as wet and cold as the soil of the churchyard that stood across the road.

The wind blew a kite's tail of the falling water from the chute across my mouth. I licked in the water and cursed Oscar, called him a hog seven times. I did not speak under my breath but out loud. No one could hear me in that empty yard. If anyone had heard me and if he did not know Oscar he would have said I was mad, shouting in that fashion. If he knew Oscar he would have said I was quite right. Everybody in the valley knew Oscar was a very dirty element.

I stared at the tall railings that the Council had planted on the wall of the churchyard opposite. I tried to count the number of spikes in those railings and gave up that job with the thought that they were many. I wondered whether those tall railings were to keep the dead voters in or the live voters out. There were many things done by that Council that I did not understand. But I was young. That I was working for a hog who spent less than one day in a hundred sober meant that I must have been very dense as well. The only bright thing I ever remember doing was to take that waterproof jacket from the house of my uncle who had just died.

(in THE SKY OF OUR LIVES, *pp. 9–10)*

The short sentences roll off this opening page of 'Oscar' with apparently artless ease, connected not by syntax but by the repetition of key words usually preceded by a demonstrative: 'a waterproof jacket . . . That jacket'; 'the "Harp" . . . that pub'; 'a lighted window . . . that window . . .

that window'; 'a dozen drunks . . . those drunks'; 'Oscar . . . that Oscar' etc. Sometimes there is repetition for the sake of antithesis: 'did not bother him . . . It bothered me'; 'if he did not know Oscar . . . If he knew Oscar'; 'to keep the dead voters in or the live voters out'. Although the sentences appear to be in first-person narration, they do not narrate events but reveal the narrator's thoughts as he surveys his dismal situation. Colloquial as it seems, the style is not bereft of imagery ('a kite's tail of the falling water') and there are striking transferred metaphors: 'The light from that window . . . had a taste'; 'There was a feel about [Oscar's voice], a slow greasy feel'. It was perhaps the lexical mannerisms which impressed themselves upon contemporary readers: people are transformed into 'voters' or 'elements', the village, into a 'zone'. The rhythm is extraordinarily terse, matching the desolation of the scene: three-quarters of the sentences end with monosyllabic words, and this is sometimes achieved by hyperbaton ('a lighted window, small'). There is a marked self-awareness in the 'I'-narrator: Lewis, the hoggish Oscar's creature, knows that he is 'very dense' to work for that 'very dirty element', but this is accompanied by a strong sense of hopelessness, shared, as it turns out, by nearly all the characters in the story.

'Oscar' contains short sections where the author takes over from the colloquial tone of the first-person narrator and the style is momentarily heightened. This high style always coincides with passages of social criticism, which are saved from mawkishness by the strong tone of indignation and the writer's inbuilt warning mechanism against sentimentality, so that he breaks the mood with a flippant phrase as can be seen in the last sentence of the following passage:

I thought Oscar was lucky indeed to be able to clear out of his head things he had said and done no more than two days before. If you have the courage that comes from never being slapped down, cheated or made hungry, you can perform this cleaning-out process and think nothing of it.

Only those whose poverty seems to have existed from the earth's beginning have to put up with being dragged below the surface by the dead chains of past years, past days. The poor hug to their hearts all the yesterdays they know have not been lived and the burden is a heavy one. But Oscar was free. He could cut afresh the tape of each new morning, and the day he marched through was a road in itself, whole and complete, attached to no navel string of before or after. Yesterday meant no more to Oscar than the past life of the farthest star to me. It was all right, for Oscar.

(*in* THE SKY OF OUR LIVES, *p. 64*)

On the thematic level, 'Oscar' exhibits the author's early and continuing fascination with the wilder fringes of human behaviour. The eponymous protagonist is indeed a monstrous composite of villainies: a savage exploiter of the poorest of his neighbours who come to pick coal on the mountain he owns, a ravisher of their womenfolk, a glutton and drunkard, he finally turns to murder just for the thrill of it:

I ought to be able to do as I like to people like that. Don't know what they live for, anyway. Sometimes I've watched them. Sometimes when a stone has come rolling down the tip, I've watched them run and duck and lie on their guts full

*stretch to get out of the stone's way, as if they had as much
to live for as a bloody king or me or somebody like that, and
sometimes I've prayed, I've watched the stone and prayed
that the stone would be smarter than them and smack their
bloody brains out, just to teach them a lesson. I ought to be
able to do as I like to them. I've often felt like that. I'd like to
kill somebody, Lewis. That's the thing to make you tingle,
I bet. To smash somebody into hell and to shout as you're
smashing. 'There you are, you poor blundering bastard. There
go your dreams and your eyes and your hopes and your arms,
all the bloody things you got that make you feel so grand,
so proud . . .'*

(*in* THE SKY OF OUR LIVES, *p. 45*)

There is no sense of surprise when Oscar is
pushed over the edge of his mountain by his
exasperated right-hand man (the narrator).

'Simeon', from the same collection of short
stories, contains less overt social criticism than
'Oscar', but it has a protagonist who is more
quietly horrible. Not only do Mr Simeon's hot
lusts cause him to assault everything in sight,
including his three daughters (two of whom bear
him sons), his young handyman (the narrator),
and his four goats; he is also revealed as a
murderer (who has buried the cadaver in the
cabbage-patch) just before he receives his own
savage quittance on the point of a breadknife
held by his youngest daughter Bess. This pen-
chant for *grand guignol* is strong in the earlier
stories and is never entirely absent from the later
works. In a television lecture in 1968 the author
himself commented on the fascination of the
criminal as a literary topic:

7

Our felons, the large and terrible legion of murderers, rapists, robbers, cast a weird light into the darker corridors of our collective memory. It is almost as if there is some nourishing absurdity in the antics of these outrageous clowns who allow their hatred, greed, boredom and a witless wish for a change of idiom to head them towards the arch-discourtesies of theft and murder. They are the sore teeth that never fail to attract the tongue of our own moral perplexity.

Although some of the London literary critics of his first collections of stories found them 'wildly improbable', Gwyn would later defend the melo-dramatic element in his work in a typical way:

In a social ambience so emphatically tainted with lunacy as that of a mining area moving into dereliction, I took even the dottiest libretto in my stride. The plots of the early and middle Verdi in which probability stands in the centre of the stage, bow-legged and gaping, I accepted as prosaic reality. As a member of the Band of Hope Junior operatic group I once played in 'Trovatore'. After years of being harassed into primness and piety by the zealots of the diaconate addressing me in Welsh, a language I did not understand, I found no difficulty in accepting that a vengeful gypsy, whose mother has been burned at the stake by a Duke, should not only wish to burn the Duke's child but actually burned her own child in error. A predilection for violence, ashes and serious mistakes overlay my entire culture.

(in PLAYS AND PLAYERS, *February 1963, p. 26)*

As well as his lifelong devotion to Italian opera, as an adolescent Gwyn was also a devotee of Victorian melodrama and the silent cinema.

Of the early works, THE DARK PHILOSOPHERS deserves the closest attention, not least because the author himself regards it as *the completest expression of what he wants to say* (reported in THE WESTERN MAIL, 7th April 1952). In this *novella* the style can be seen to reach a 'second state', in which imagery is more developed, exaggeration and repetition are used to more comic effect, and occasional verbal and mental side-steps occur in almost Joycean fashion:

Emmanuel's parents had been poor people from the Terraces. When they died, the schoolmaster had pointed out to Mr Dalbie, the managing director of the colliery in which we worked, what a fine bright-eyed promising look there was about Emmanuel. Mr Dalbie was a hard man. He had three wooden sheds built at the back of his large house. One was for his coal, the second for his wood and the third for his pity.

He was not usually interested in anyone unless that person happened to be looking bright-eyed and promising over the task of digging coal for Mr Dalbie. But he must have wanted a change or a rest when Emmanuel was pointed out to him. He may have left the door of that third shed off the latch one griping night in winter, and glimpsed the slow procession of our more faltering comrades making their way from the pit to their hillside homes. Or, more believable, even the hardest skull might find it difficult to prevent the thought of a young orphan driving a straight hole through to its soft core.

Old orphans did badly in the Terraces, but young ones still had a fighting chance especially if, as in the case of Emmanuel, there was a schoolmaster doing propaganda on his behalf. Mr Dalbie paid the boy's way through school and college, and provided him on graduation with one of the valley's most commodious pulpits.

Then Mr Dalbie had a shock. He had had so little active experience of being benevolent that he created around his services to Emmanuel a private legend of pure gold. He

expected, if not a daily salaam, at least a song of complaisant gratitude from the boy who, had it not been for this incalculable spasm of fondness, would have gone into the pit and received a full blast of shot from one of the two barrels of the gun that Mr Dalbie handled in his double function of pit manager and Justice of the little Peace we knew in our valley.
(*in* THE SKY OF OUR LIVES, *pp. 94–95*)

Digression now becomes increasingly important, as in the following passage where no sooner are we introduced to Idomeneo's Italian café than there is a brief reminiscence of another South Welsh focal point, the Working Men's Institute:

Our new meeting place in the evenings was the refreshment and confectionery shop of Idomeneo Faracci, an Italian, whose shop was on the third Terrace, not far from the Library and Institute, where we had now taken out fresh membership cards for the sake of attending lectures and borrowing books. This Institute was a useful place for all voters whose minds liked to dwell on those serious topics with which the Terraces slopped over, and there was room there, too, for those whose maximum in the way of mental action was billiards, ludo or just coming in out of the cold.

The Institute had several rooms set aside for the playing of simple games, and these rooms were much used by backward types whose speciality was horseplay or sitting in a sort of trance at the portals of puberty with their ears to the keyhole, and learning the facts of life at second-hand and fainting every so often from pure surprise.
(*in* THE SKY OF OUR LIVES, *pp. 104–05*)

This art of digression is later developed into a means of instantly capturing the feeling of a place or the essence of a person.

10

Despite its gloomy title, THE DARK PHILOSOPHERS already shows off Gwyn's zany humour in almost mature form. It is not only to be found in incongruity of situation, though there is plenty of that, and in the comic attitudes, but it is ingrained in the very texture of the writing: the carefully placed adverbial phrase, such as 'in a sort of trance' or 'every so often' at the end of the passage just quoted, the affective use of adjectives, *'simple* games', *'pure* surprise', the comically extended metaphors, 'at the portals of puberty with their ears to the keyhole'.

All the stock narrative elements of Gwyn's works are already discernible in THE DARK PHILOSOPHERS: the Rhondda setting in 'the Terraces' during the Depression of the thirties, the group of friends, until recently unemployed, who meet in the Library and Institute or in the Italian café where they listen to records of Italian opera or have fierce socialist discussions. There are certain differences to note between this work and the earlier stories: the setting is not now the Rhondda of the twenties' slump, but the late thirties, when employment is beginning to return to the valleys; the 'I'-narrator of 'Oscar' and 'Simeon' is replaced by 'We'—the group of friends—; the general crudity of expression of the stories is confined to passages of direct speech, and the high metaphoric style is to the fore. The protagonist, Emmanuel, far from being a subhuman lout or monster like the anti-heroes of the earlier tales, is a bright orphan who makes the most of the opportunities offered him. Safely ensconced in his pulpit, the Rev. Emmanuel denounces *the overlong hours, brutalising toil and poor housing which were converting such places as the Terraces into catchment areas for oafs and cretins* (p. 95). The pressures put on him to abandon his political crusade and the girl he loves, and his steady conversion into a pillar of the establishment, are wryly charted. The inexorable slow stain of the world on any spokesman of the proletariat becomes one of the principal themes in the Thomas *œuvre*, and it forms the chief preoccupation of the narrators in this *novella*. The monster-type also makes a brief appearance, in the character of Hector, *A backward element who looked like an ape and acted like some animal that has not been found yet and has not been named for that reason; unless you want to take a short cut and call it Hector* (p. 143). The Rev. Emmanuel, however, can be viewed as more subtly monstrous than the brutish Hector; there is a cold-blooded self-interest in the minister's behaviour which is not redeemed by his faltering attempts late in life to return to the paths of socialism and love, which are crowned by his final spectacular twitch into death when possessed of the *hwyl* in the pulpit. The abandonment of Mrs Radnor, and her struggles to bring up her daughter decently, bring out Gwyn's highest gifts of *saeva indignatio*:

For all who had lived in the Terraces we had a kind of love, a comradeship that has beauty for having no axe to grind, and that love made us quick to sense the coming in or going out of life. To all those who have lived without wealth, importance, purpose or consolation, the simple act of living acquires a meaning that increases to a point when we can never describe the feelings we have before the simple act of dying.

Above us, in that small bedroom, there was ending in a silence that was sweet and intelligent to the ears that listened,

12

a brief story of great effort that had proceeded to failure as naturally as a thirsty animal would proceed to water. You may read the story of poverty, oppression and human failure in learned books and feel your brain burn at the wretched spectacle of the stupid tormenting the weak, but try sitting on an iron bench on a dark night meditating upon the death that is shortly to come, a few yards away, to one of stupidity's victims, who has put more intelligence, strength and valour into trying to win a civilised standard of decency for herself and a child, than ever any of history's revered baboons put into the exploitation of their kingdoms, strip mills or coal mines, and yet dies without any outward evidence of having made anything but a hell of a mess of it, and your brain will do something more than burn. It will have the grey, dusty fragility of coke.

(*in* THE SKY OF OUR LIVES, *pp. 168–69*)

The similarity of the opening of the two sentences in the first paragraph: 'For all who had lived in the Terraces . . .', 'To all those who have lived without wealth . . .', and the long central sentence of the second paragraph, have more to do with the art of oratory than that of rhetorical writing, as can be seen by the direct appeal to a listener: 'You may read . . . feel your brain burn . . . try sitting . . . your brain will do . . .'; the sudden colloquial tone of 'a hell of a mess of it' which points up the surrounding lofty phrases; the grave deceleration in the final short statement.

THE ALONE TO THE ALONE (published in 1947) has a very similar narrative framework: the four semi-employed friends, who are the narrators, this time attempt to come to the aid of Eurona, who *was very dark and had a face that was full of deep, struggling dreams . . . She looked, as far as her clothes went, as though she had been pulled through brambles and then pushed through a thin tube* (p. 14). She falls disastrously in love with a bus conductor, Rollo, who is the leading local Casanova: *Rollo had only to wink and a maiden would fall and he winked so often it was getting difficult to see a perpendicular maiden in the Terraces any more* (p. 23). But the real protagonist is Eurona's father, Morris, whom Glyn Jones has excellently described as *that marvellous comic study of a man completely demoralized, degutted and reduced to near imbecility by the savage social and industrial climate in which he has to live* (THE DRAGON HAS TWO TONGUES, p. 121). So terrified by life is he that he resists all attempts by the four narrators to get him to assert his rights. This novel received much more critical acclaim in Britain and the United States than THE DARK PHILOSOPHERS, no doubt because it was the first of Gwyn's books to be published by a well established London publisher; it was also the only one of his works that came seriously close to being converted into a Broadway musical. It is clear that most of the contemporary critics did not know what to make of the novel and they came out with some odd judgements: *Not that Mr Thomas has any great pretensions to style; indeed, the language too often runs off the rails into obscurity or meaninglessness* (P. H. Newby in THE LISTENER, 25th September 1947); *whiffs of remembrance of the best of Belloc and Chesterton* (Wilson Keith in THE CORNHILL MAGAZINE, January 1948); *Karl Marx in the rarified form once known as Christian Socialism* (Lewis Gannett in THE NEW YORK HERALD TRIBUNE, 6th May 1947); *something like* THE GRAPES OF WRATH, *but funny* (Donald B. Willard in THE BOSTON DAILY GLOBE, 15th January 1948). The critic who understood the work best was a fellow Anglo-Welsh writer, Professor Gwyn Jones:

It is quite unlike any other novel about the same subject. The theme of social injustice is in every paragraph, but the treatment is comic, and more specifically ironic. Nothing could be more misleading than to summarize the 'plot', for the narrative element is little more than an excuse for the display of Mr Thomas's virtuosity as a humorist. On the whole he is here a kindly one, and even his indignation is checked by a sense of the ludicrous and the helpless in men . . . THE ALONE TO THE ALONE is a book which bears fresh witness to a new and striking talent among us. The main faults are the deliberate greyness and shroudlike texture, the refusal to differentiate character other than by externals, and from time to time a maundering style. The merits are the consistent vision, the power of creating the writer's own world, the power and compression of the style at its best, and the humour . . . It is the kind of humour which is founded on the serious, the solemnly incredible, the incongruously realistic.

(WELSH REVIEW, *Summer 1947*)

In 1947 Gwyn had already begun work on his longest and most ambitious novel, ALL THINGS BETRAY THEE. At first he had thought of entitling it MY ROOT ON EARTH, and in its first form it consisted of 170,000 words. The publisher's reader, however, not understanding that digression was an important element in Gwyn's style, wanted the digressions weeded out, to 'make the story much tauter and more exciting'. ALL THINGS BETRAY THEE is not an historical novel in the accepted sense, for the author uses the Riots at Merthyr Tydfil in 1831 as a vehicle for the motifs he had earlier elaborated in the Rhondda of the twenties and thirties: the irontown of 'Moonlea' is the successor of 'the Terraces' and the fore-runner of 'Ferncleft', 'Meadow Prospect' and 'Belmont'. The characters are more fully worked out than in the earlier stories: the narrator is now a deep-thinking and foot-loose harpist, who inclines more to the solitude of the rural North, which he idealises, than to the political and social imbroglios of the irontown. He provides the key to interpreting the theme of the novel: the artist's reluctance to do more than observe the struggles of his fellows—perhaps a reflection of the author's own dilemma. The harpist's friend is the near-hero, John Simon Adams, who is the Dic Penderyn figure; he demonstrates an astonishing power of leadership over the prolet-ariat, but possesses an optimistic innocence which blinds him to the real evil genius of the oppressive classes and which prevents his taking effective action at the vital moment. He represents the 'failed leader' theme which recurs under different forms in Gwyn's later work. The oppressors include Richard Penbury, the ironmaster with the romantic and crypto-radical streak, his cold-blooded but sensual daughter Helen, the monstrous baker Lemuel Stevens, who has sold his soul to the class enemy out of greed and fright, Mr Bowen the hypocritical divine, Lord Plimmon the entirely eighteenth-century aristo-crat, Radcliffe the iron-willed works manager, and Jarvis the ingratiating lawyer.

As he describes how Alan Leigh, the harpist-narrator, becomes ever more enmeshed in the preparations for the workers' rebellion against the ironmaster's lockout, the author resorts to a surging poetic style which reaches a climax when the harpist watches in the gloom from the South Mountain for the arrival of the workers' contingents from the Southern valleys:

Then below me, five great veins of redness pressed to the surface of the night. The legions were coming up from the south, men bearing torches in their ranks, making for the foot of the mountain on which I stood. I looked fascinated at the broad streams of brightness that came closer, clearer. John Simon had been right. In the hearts and minds of the folk who had been gathered in from their quiet fields to labour in other ways between those hills there had been a ripeness I had not seen, a fullness I had not felt. But it was I in my tiny acre of pride and sufficiency who was coming to flower, very slowly, testing, suspecting, even hating the petals that would grow ruthlessly into the pattern of a more merciful, more exacting, more hazardous understanding.

As the first wave of torches touched the foot of the South Mountain and began their slow, orderly climb I began to cry and shout, exultantly, like a madman, as if all the lovely, loving gentleness of man on earth had been gathered up into one symbol and presented to me for the first time.

(ALL THINGS BETRAY THEE, *pp. 175–76*)

This extended metaphor for the five torch-lit processions coming up the valleys from the south and converging on Moonlea begins with the 'great veins of redness' and 'the broad streams of brightness' which coincide with the petals of the flower of political understanding unfolding in the onlooker's mind; they form a floriferous symbol which is 'gathered up' and 'presented' to him in this euphoric climax.

When, six pages later, the riot is savagely put

down by the militia and John Simon Adams recognises the error of his fatal reluctance to use arms, the tone is switched to one of bitter disillusion, which is maintained almost to the novel's close. Yet there, in the final paragraph, some critics have seen a hint of future proletarian victory:

Night had fallen completely when I began the climb of Arthur's Crown, walking up the same path I had descended on my way into Moonlea. On its summit I looked down. There below me was the house of Penbury, big, smiling, living with light. I turned, walking away from Moonlea, yet eternally towards Moonlea, full of a strong, ripening, unanswerable bitterness, feeling in my fingers the promise of a new, enormous music.

(ALL THINGS BETRAY THEE, *p. 318*)

But both author and reader know that similar events were to take place in the mining valleys almost a century later which would again end in defeat for the working class. The 'new, enormous music' which is promised seems to refer to the artist's new political commitment. Gone is the false dream of a rural glen in the North. Support for this interpretation can be found at the beginning of the final chapter, when the harpist-narrator is discussing the failure of the riot with Jameson, the revolutionary tavern-keeper. John Simon Adams, whom the harpist saw 'as something projecting from my own self', has been hanged, his fellow leader, Longridge, cornered and reputed killed by a troop of dragoons: *They bit at something that was unripe, bitter. They should have waited. They were in too much of a hurry . . . They had too little cunning* (p. 311). Jameson gives him a more

18

optimistic view:

'We state the facts, now softly, now loudly. The next time it will be softly for our best voices have ceased to speak. The silence and the softness will ripen. The lost blood will be made again. The chorus will shuffle out of its filthy aching corners and return. The world is full of voices, practising for the great anthem but hardly ever heard. We've been privileged. We've had our ears full of the singing. Silence will never be absolute for us again.'

'That's so', I said, looking up at him. 'That's so. The silence will never again be absolute. The back of our own dumbness will have been broken and it must have been a granite sort of spine while it lasted. But the ears of John Simon, that once could hear music in every voice, on every wind, are stopped. Will that fact ever cease to make me sick, a stranger to myself and the whole of life, in those moments when it takes me by the thumbs and strings me up?'

'The fact will grow into you. Finally it will be all of you, your new root.'

'I hear much talk of roots . . . I'd better go. You've been kind, Mr. Jameson. Is it safe for me to go now?'

(ALL THINGS BETRAY THEE, *pp. 311–12*)

'The new root' can be seen to be equivalent to the 'new, enormous music' mentioned in the last sentence of the novel: the harpist's political commitment. And the likelihood that this corresponds to the novelist's *engagement* is confirmed by our knowledge that he had earlier considered MY ROOT ON EARTH for the novel's title.

At the time of its publication, the work had a mixed reception, perhaps because the publisher's blurb had led the critics to expect a traditional kind of historical novel: *There is no sense of period,*

19

no feeling of an earlier age (BOOKS OF TODAY, June 1949), *he has infused his book with modern twists of speech and turns of thought so that his novel seems timeless and unreal instead of being anchored to any particular epoch* (Orville Prescott in THE NEW YORK TIMES, 26th July 1949); though P. H. Newby recognised that this may have been the author's intention: *has not set out to transcribe reality, he has transfigured it with all the rhetoric at his command* (THE LISTENER, June 1949), and it was also better understood by Henry Treece, Howard Spring and Professor Idris Parry. It was popular enough to receive a Book Society recommendation, and the film rights were sold, though two separate projects to make it into a film came to nought. With the advantage of nearly thirty years' perspective, it is probable that many of us would not wish seriously to dissent from Glyn Jones's judgement of ALL THINGS BETRAY THEE: *The book has for me every good thing of which Gwyn Thomas is capable, and marks the peak of his achievement in the field of the novel, as distinct from the play or the short story. It is less shapely perhaps than* THE ALONE TO THE ALONE, *or than* THE LOVE MAN *for that matter, but it is given a sort of organic unity by being written around an obsessive contemporary theme, namely the class struggle and the place of the artist in it* (THE DRAGON HAS TWO TONGUES, p. 115). The American writer Howard Fast saw it as *so great an advance in terms of realism, in terms of understanding and historical perspective, that its positive qualities far outweigh its faults* (LITERATURE AND REALITY, p. 67).

All readers of Gwyn's books are fascinated by the originality and spontaneity of his style and wonder how it arose. Glyn Jones remarks that *His writing has always seemed to me only a slightly more condensed version of his brilliant conversation* (THE DRAGON HAS TWO TONGUES, p. 109). The author himself has said: '*I have never had to lash myself to a desk to write. It has always been compulsive with me, like the crying of a child. But this can rob writing of its cunning and I have not written with enough concern for the people who are going to interpret it*' (quoted by Trevor Fishlock in THE TIMES, 23rd November 1974). No one who has ever had the joy of being in Gwyn's company will doubt that he writes just as he speaks. South Walians who read his books continually catch echoes of their own dialect of English, and more specifically, echoes of the terse and witty speech of the Rhondda Valleys. Although his parents and the oldest children spoke Welsh, Gwyn was brought up in an English-orientated household, strongly radical in its politics like the community to which it belonged. That community was a unique social occurrence in every respect: on to the few remaining sheep-farming families of the eighteenth century, there were added Welshmen of peasant stock from the Western counties, slatemen from the North, many families from South-West England and Irish immigrants. A rich and explosive racial mix, attracted by the mining jobs in the nineteenth and early twentieth centuries, they were to be ruined by the sharp decline in world demand for Welsh steam coal in the twenties and further impoverished by the slump in the thirties, until at one point 42 per cent of the male employable population were out of work. Not that they had ever been faintly prosperous, but they were now to know a grinding poverty which pitched them, as Gwyn puts it, *on to a lower social level than the ancient serfs* (THE DARK PHILOSOPHERS, in THE SKY OF OUR

21

Lives, p. 141).

Gwyn's grandparents had emigrated to the
United States where his father Walter Morgan
Thomas was born in 1872. Although trained as a
cabinet-maker by his father, Walter Morgan
Thomas went to work as an ostler in the pits of
the Rhondda, where he settled and brought up
his large family of eight sons and four daughters.
Not only was the father well known locally as a
raconteur, but, of Gwyn's elder brothers, Walter
and Dillwyn especially showed great power of
inventive wit. Walter preceded Gwyn to university, taking a brilliant degree in modern languages
at the University College of South Wales, Cardiff,
and became one of the great teachers of his
generation. He too has a most original way of
speaking and writing, not dissimilar to Gwyn's,
in which rich imagery replaces the cliché. During
their adolescence, the household, although poor
because of the father's continuous unemployment, was bright with intellectual and political
chitchat and loud with music. They were keen
devotees of the cinema, particularly of the Marx
brothers and early Bogart films, and their reading
was very wide ranging, O. Henry, Runyan and
Perelman being special favourites. It may be that
on the fertile base of the Rhondda speech a kind
of family ideolect grew among the Thomas
children, which Gwyn nurtured to a point at
which it became peculiarly his.

II

Between 1950 and 1960, although he was still a full-time teacher, Gwyn Thomas entered his most prolific period, writing six novels, two collections of short stories and twelve plays for radio. The first of the novels of this middle period was THE WORLD CANNOT HEAR YOU, which, unlike his other early novels, has a tripartite structure. The setting is once more the Rhondda of the 1930s and the narrators are the same group of friends as in THE ALONE TO THE ALONE. The pathetic protagonist is Omri Hemlock, one of two North Welsh brothers who have come south to Meadow Prospect to find work in the pits. Omri is unaffected when his wife runs off with the Council painter at the start of the novel:

Whatever calamity dealt Omri a clip, there was no answering anger; only a slight shrug and a message to the calamity that he, Omri, after a good deal of futile standing up and catching it from a wide range of missiles was now ready to lie down, be still and have done with all protest and strife (p. 6).

He fails to reckon, however, with the ambitions of his brother Bodvan:

He was smaller again than Omri but he was a walking glow of energy, the nearest we will ever come to Napoleon in this essentially modest strip of the Celtic fringe where the rates are so high they make everybody look short. Bodvan had the kind of appetite for ownership and power which would have allowed him to pick up the world and suck it dry of juice like

23

*an orange if he had the opportunity and time to get a grip.
But Bodvan was in the wrong place and the wrong epoch.
In all man's experience of seeing property cornered never
have the corners been more sharply defined and defended than
in Meadow Prospect. Pits, two iron works, shops, houses had
been assigned their pockets as rigidly as the stars their
constellations and the owners had no wish to be re-arranging
the heavens, not even for such an eager voter as Bodvan.
He overdid eagerness. Any man who goes about with a light
in his eye clearly telling life that he expects much from it is
asking for trouble. Life, which nourishes itself on darkness,
and hates to have the shaking flare of torches thrown on its
threadbare years, will notice the light in the voter's eye and
will take pleasure in dowsing it.*

(THE WORLD CANNOT HEAR YOU, *p. 7*)

The remainder of the first part recounts Bodvan's
ingratiation with Mr Sylvester Strang, the local
landowner and idealistic social worker, his acqui-
sition of the stoniest tract of mountainside above
Meadow Prospect, and his and Omri's efforts to
cultivate it, until they are cheated by the local
arch-rogue and lecher, Picton Gethin, and finally
ruined by natural means:

*The ruin of the Hemlocks was soon complete. In the late
summer and autumn the whole family of calamity called in
and made itself at home. Four different varieties of blight
came to a fullness of knowledge and strength within their four
walls and row upon row of long-tended produce perished as it
grew. Then came the belt of memorable rainstorms. The
mountain stream near the homestead switched from its course,
boiled in fury over the skimpy topsoil of the brothers'
settlement and ruined beyond hope of decent restoration the
interior of their bleak home. Then one October night, a wind
that seemed to have been saving its spite towards us since the*

very beginning of the Industrial Revolution came howling through the hills, its programme no less than to shave off every sprout of life that darkened the earth.

(THE WORLD CANNOT HEAR YOU, *p. 99*)

Whereas the manipulators of Omri in the first part were his brother Bodvan and Mr Strang, in the second Picton Gethin takes over. The only object of Omri's affections earlier had been his horse Bloom, which was worked to its death by Picton. Now he conceives a kind of love for a fellow road-maker called Octavius Pym:

Omri did not come with us into this establishment. He remained with Octavius Pym and it was good to see these two voters together, their quiet modest hearts interlocked in what seemed to be a most pleasant idyll, great listeners, great smilers who could stand equally delighted at the sight of a moving cloud, a flight of birds, a roll of grassland or the twitch of yearning on some defeated face. They achieved a great contentment in the quietness of the mountain road that linked the valleys where so much of our work was done. They looked like brothers. Both were short, grizzled, addicted to the wearing of oilskin hats and neither had any love for wearing the false teeth which they possessed. They said that these contraptions rubbed their gums crazy, having been clumsily made by a dentist who seemed not to care whether the world did any biting or not. But our belief was that Octavius and Omri felt that it was arrogant and boastful to go flashing such a zone of bought whiteness from the middle of the face. They ate meagrely and the mice in their house must have carried as many banners of protests against the poorness of the régime as we had done through the streets of Meadow Prospect. We urged upon them that it would be better for them both if they came in with us at Mrs Wallace's but they just shook their heads inside their oilskin hats as if they had found some small

25

experience which they wished to enjoy while they could.
(THE WORLD CANNOT HEAR YOU, *p. 106*)

The idyll is soon over when Octavius Pym's grasping sister carts him off to her boarding house in Pembrokeshire.

The obsessive attentions now showered on Omri by Picton Gethin resemble those shown by a stoat to a rabbit, and after this second bout of manipulation, Omri ends up in hospital, a mental and physical wreck. The third part recounts Omri's extraordinarily unsuccessful attempts at self-renewal through his ill-conceived passion for Delphine Stringer of The Three Star Mission. Although social criticism is still present in this novel, it is more muted than in the earlier works. We have here a highly comic study of human weakness, and the set-pieces reach new heights of hilarity in describing Omri's attempts to be an insulting barrow-boy, to achieve a lifelong ambition to sing 'On with the Motley' at an amateur concert, to take succour to flooded villagers in a leaky boat, and to woo Delphine Stringer by paying for the Mission children's annual outing to the seaside. The joyous finale provided by this last description is perhaps the funniest in all Gwyn's work; here is part of the account of the hiring of the bathing costumes:

We entered the hutches and put on our costumes. They were old, thin and stretched down to a remarkable length.

'This garment of mine', we heard Ewart Pugh say thoughtfully, 'was last worn by a Zeppelin.'

We all came forth. We made an impressive group. All the costumes had given up the ghost of their original seemliness and the bottoms came lower than halfway down the leg. In Omri's case, one foot at least was reached. Ewart, with his leanness, was not much better off. His costume had breadth as well as length and he had to be nimble and alert to keep the thing on him at all. He stalked up to the counter.

'What kind of conspiracy is this, boy?' he asked. 'Here we are looking like a guild of blue bloody Druids. Now let's see something that comes within a foot of the frame, boy.'

'That's all you'll get here. The boss of this place hasn't bought a new costume since the big strike when he lost all confidence in you elements from the hills. This type of cloth has a lot of give. That's a good thing in cloth. We never have any complaints. Take it or leave it. I picked these especially long because that's what you wanted, isn't it?'

'What do you mean?'

'You came down with that Mission, didn't you?'

'Yes, we're with them.'

'So you're holy. You wouldn't want anything tight to put your paraphernalia in the headlines. You boys have gone beyond that sort of thing.'

'That's right', said Omri, 'I like a bit of slackness.'

This brought the man's attention sharply on to Omri. Omri had left his wig in the cubicle and the shroudlike effect of the costume threw the bareness of his head into terrible relief. The man leaned over the counter and looked at Omri suspiciously.

'Who's that bald-headed joker? He wasn't among those who paid. What happened to the voter with the red mop? Are you trying to trick me?'

'Go back for your wig, Omri', said Ewart, 'Let's amaze this element all we can.'

Omri went back into the cubicle and returned fitting his wig on.

'A lewd lot', said the man, 'Especially you voters from missions. I've always said it. You come down here just to let it rip.'

We stepped forward to have a formal debate with the man on what a wig should have to do with lewdness but Omri said he was getting cold standing about on the stone floor. We made our way out of the building down a flight of rough granite steps. Omri had kept his wig on.

'What in God's name do you want that thatch on for if you are going to bathe? You proved to that attendant that you are not Jekyll and his ginger twin. Now you can leave it off. You're going in altogether too much for pomp.'

'Oh I don't know. Thinking it over, Denzil, I believe I'll keep it on. I don't like the way Miss Delphine was looking at me in the marquee. I've got to look my best now.'

'You look odd, as if you had been sent ashore by the fish.'

'Anyway it's warm. And the wind gets at me terribly in this costume. The only things that are touching me are the shoulder straps.'

We walked into the cold water. We noticed that Delphine and a small cloud of children had walked over the sands to watch. She was looking intently at Omri as if she had received instructions from Calvin Kiddy to keep an eye on Omri from now on and bring back a progress report.

The nearness of Delphine galvanised Omri. He started shouting sportingly at us, beating his chest and daring us to strike out and touch the Devon coast with both hands before coming back. He laid himself on the water and kicked his legs violently. He shot forward but the costume stayed behind. The same thing happened with Caradoc Dando and the sea around us seemed to be covering itself with big blue stains. We gathered around them as they crouched in their nakedness and stood there while we helped float them back into their shrouds. Delphine on the beach turned away in disgust as if Omri had been having that costume made to measure and then stretched for months past in readiness for just this caper of publicly casting his slough.

(THE WORLD CANNOT HEAR YOU, *pp. 257–59*)

As this passage illustrates, the author's style has entered its full maturity and assuredness. His greater use of comic sobriquets in this novel emphasises the fact that humour is now in command: Naboth Jinks the Pinks, Mathew Sewell the Sotto, Edwin Pugh the Pang, Peredur Parry the Pittance. Glyn Jones (THE DRAGON HAS TWO TONGUES, p. 111) has already commented on Gwyn's use for comic effect of the many non-Welsh, immigrant surnames which occur in the Rhondda placed alongside Welsh, historical, biblical or aristocratic christian names; in this novel we can note Salathiel Cull, Jethro Manley, Kitchener Draisey, Fawcett Stringer, Caradoc Dando, Mathias Purcell, Jonquil Toms and the three brothers Windsor, Balmoral and Buckingham Cann. Note should also be made of the names for institutions: the Mafeking Club (ex-servicemen's), the Birchtown Bantams (football club), The Col (Coliseum Cinema), the Cottage of Content (rehabilitation centre), Yearn (residential college) and the Black Meadow (the cemetery); and the poetic names for taverns: The Ingle, The Moss for the Stones. The high comedy is sustained by the strange religious sects invented by the author:

'These are the Knockers', said Denzil. 'They are a quieter lot altogether than some of the others . . . talking is not important for the Knockers.'
  'Whom do they knock?'
  'Nobody.'
  'What's the board for?'
  'To knock on . . . Listen. These Knockers have seen things darkening for a long time past . . . They believe that somewhere in the whole wilderness of man's wanting there is

a door. To that door there is no key but it waits ready to answer the one particular rhythm of yearning which will strike love and pity into its hinges . . . At a certain point in the service they all rap on their knocking boards.'

'*And they expect the door to paradise to swing open in such a place as this where even the bum-bailiffs have been knocking their knuckles off in vain for the last fifty years?'*

'*They are not too literal. When they beat that tattoo on their boards, they are just serving life notice that it should now stop acting the sour fool and start smiling more genially at the voters.'*

(THE WORLD CANNOT HEAR YOU, *pp. 14–15*)

All these comic features are continued in NOW LEAD US HOME (1952), the starting-point for which, as the author explicitly states, was William Randolph Hearst's purchase of St Donat's Castle during the 1930s. The setting is Ferncleft, now placed only three miles from the coast where Glimley Castle stands. The American millionaire purchaser is Mr August Slezacher, *a vendor of military accessories.* The time seems to have moved forward to the immediate post-Second World War period, in view of the mention of 'atomic burn stains' and 'atom proof igloos' (p. 147), though the characters' attitudes are those of the thirties. The narrator, Bartholomew Tull, accompanied by his friends Mark Lane and Hughie Purcell, describes the comic interaction between Mr Slezacher and the town of Ferncleft, their diametrically opposed political and industrial views, and their ultimate brief compatibility in human terms. There are no heroes or heroines in the usual sense, but a remarkable gallery of characters is spread out before us, the novelty being a revolutionary woman bus conductor,

Bronnie Vaughan, who shakes up the town council and enters spiritedly into the political discussions in Ildebrando Galuppi's café. The plot is not important or elaborate: it concerns Luther Lecky and Caswallon Marsh, a delicate and womanly pair, who pay religious but not over-zealous court to Edwina Lane, the local beauty. Much to their relief she runs off to London to become a singer, but ends up as a waitress and a whore. Her sudden return in a consumptive state alarms them, but delights Mr Slezacher, who finds her irresistible, and her operatic death provides the dénouement. All this is no more than a frame on which the author hangs highly comic scenes: the rehearsal of *La Traviata,* the civic tea, the performance of *La Bohème,* the druidic pageant held in the castle grounds. A sign that these scenes are much more important than the frame is the discrepancy between the fact that one opera is rehearsed (pp. 60–66) and another is performed (pp. 118–35). Almost without the reader noticing, the author soon reconciles this inconsistency by inventing retrospectively a per-formance of *La Traviata* on the night following that of *La Bohème* (pp. 138 and 151). I nany case it is appropriate that the two operas with fatally consumptive heroines should be sung, since they provide a link with Edwina Lane's self-willed death-bed scene, which results in Glimley Castle being made over to the narrators, who wisely pass it quickly on to the County Council as a convalescent home.

Again we find poetic pub names: 'The Dew on the Dust', 'The Sea's Old Sound' (later called 'The Ancient Sound of the Sea'). And an interesting *sad, prophetic sect, the Children of the Minimum, who believe that the whole world is going to blow up or melt between now and 1960 . . . It's a peculiar sect, a bit of Trappism, a bit of Buddhism, laced with a bit of cretinism. They go for days drinking nothing but water, eating nothing but bread and not talking (pp. 12 and 160).*

Music is always an important element in Gwyn's novels and arises naturally in the narration as indeed it did in the Rhondda community. On occasion it is an integral part of the action, as in this passage from the end of THE DARK PHILOSOPHERS:

The procession made its way up the tree-lined drive on the other side of the valley. Willie walked at my side, looking tight, bulging, as if someone had tied him tight with string from head to foot. I whistled the duet from 'Tosca' that Willie liked and it acted on him straightaway as if a knife had flashed up from the ground to his head cutting every inch of the twine that bound him. He started to cry worse than a baby. We pushed him to the side of the roadway and for a minute after we could hear him crying among the trees like some new kind of bird that once lived among men.

(in THE SKY OF OUR LIVES, *pp. 204–5)*

In the earlier novels there are also scenes of concerts, of people singing around a piano or listening to gramophone records. In NOW LEAD US HOME, as we have seen, the two operas that are performed have, for the first time in Gwyn's work, a thematic connexion with the plot. It is not surprising, therefore, that the two radio plays that were transmitted in 1952, THE ORPHEANS and GAZOOKA, are entirely based on music. The first describes the alarming adventures of the Meadow

Prospect choir which had made its first appearance in THE ALONE TO THE ALONE. The second is a splendid evocation of the jazz bands which flowered in the valleys of South Wales (and which are flourishing again in some areas). GAZOOKA is the most perfect of the author's radio plays and it captures the hot summer of the General Strike in 1926 better than any documentary. Here is the opening of the radio script:

(Faintly, two drums and three or four gazookas playing 'Swanee'. It approaches, grows louder, then fades away again.)

Narrator: And to my ears, whenever that tune is played, the brave ghosts march again, and my eyes and senses are full of the wonder they knew in the months of that long idle sunlit summer of 1926. By the beginning of June the hills were bulging with a clearer loveliness than they had ever had before. No smoke rose from the great chimneys to write messages on the sky to sadden and puzzle with shadow the minds of the young. The endless journeys of trams on the inclines, loaded on the upward run and empty on the down, ceased to rattle through the night and mark our dreams. The parade of nailed boots on the pavements at dawn fell silent, and day after glorious day came up over hills that had been restored by a quirk of social conflict to the calm which they had lost a hundred years before. When the school holidays came we took to the mountain tops, joining the liberated pit ponies who were gaining a new sight, a new confidence, a new joy among the ferns on the broad plateaus. That was the picture for us who were young. For our fathers and mothers, there was the inclosing fence of hinted fears, fear of hunger, fear of defeat. And then, out of the quietness and the golden light, partly to ease their fret, a new excitement was born.

The carnivals and the jazz bands.

Rapture can sprout in the oddest places and it certainly sprouted then and there. We formed bands by the dozen, great lumps of beauty and precision, a hundred men and more in each, blowing out their marching songs on their gazookas as they paraded straight as soldiers up and down the valleys, amazing and deafening us all, each band done up in the uniform of some remote character never before seen in Meadow Prospect: Foreign Legionaries, Chinamen, Carabinieri, Grenadiers, Gauchos, or what we thought these performers looked like. There was even one group of lads living up on the cold slopes of Mynydd Coch, who did themselves up as Eskimos, but they were liquidated because even Mathew Sewell the Sotto, our leading maestro and musical adviser, couldn't think up a suitable theme song for boys dressed as delegates from the Arctic. And with the bands too came the fierce disputes inseparable from any attempt to promote a little beauty on this planet, the too hasty crowding of chilled men around its small precious flame. A new neurosis shuddered into being: Cythraul Gazookas.

It was as a result of these radio plays that Gwyn's work became much more widely known among ordinary people in Wales and outside. There grew up a Thomas following, who excitedly awaited the publication of each new book and who found it a new and rare experience to laugh out loud and uproariously at the printed page. All the works of the early fifties were well received by the critics, although one or two wondered why he did not move on to a new setting or a new period. He did not usually pay too much attention to the comments of London or New York critics, but he did feel it necessary to explain what he was about when the criticism came from nearer home. On 27th June 1952, THE BARRY HERALD published two letters which were quite eulogistic about his work, one of them from a former pupil, but they spurred the author into replying with an important statement about his literary pre-occupations and intentions—so important that I quote it *in extenso*:

My first ten or fifteen years, lived on the steepening slope of a crippled economy and a weirdly unlovely social context, among a people of unique passion, kindliness and wit, are the compost heap from which arose the materials I have used in my writing. In this regard I am utterly subjective, or if you please, selfish. I write with as little thought of the ulterior significance or the commercial value of my work as the lad who drew the bulls at Altamira. This has exposed me to some advantages and to some dangers. It enabled me to assemble from quite unlikely materials a small private world of expression in which there would be room not merely for a comic vision of what men and women do but also for the anger and pity which, even in my mellowing middle-age, have not grown much less sharp . . .

The experience of a people hardens in layers. The immediate moment is simple endurance and that in turn is pressed by time into a mineral of collective memory, sometimes base, sometimes precious. The artist's job is to go underground and work at its extraction. He works in the dark, contracting his own vocational ailments of mental astygmatism and bandiness of the moral legs; he often confuses slag with diamond, but the obstinate zeal with which he continues to haul the stuff up into the light of day is often heroic, always commendable.

The critic's task is to assay the successive samples. If there is, in the load of dross dumped at his feet by the journeyman, even an ounce of glittering ore, some completely revealed and expressed truth, he must be there to bring it forth and exhibit it in a frame of sympathetic interpretation . . .

The fact that the Rhondda gave me an unlosable tincture

need not be exaggerated. My aim is to write morality-plays in which the physical features and affiliations of the players will be less and less material . . . As for the morality of these plays, it is that of a frank, hopeful libertarianism. I despise the mouldering credos of despair and self-seclusion that have fallen like a mortal dandruff on the pate of our literati. I grew up among people who in the face of the most damnable and destructive adversity yet managed to sing their songs of resistant, rebellious belief in their own creative power and goodness. I keep singing with them until I drop . . . I would add that one man can hope to comment usefully and originally on but one tiny fragment of his time. My mind is perhaps tethered like a goat to the '20's' and '30's', the time of boyhood and young manhood. It is the wonderment of those years, bursting with fresh daily force in one's face that is the everlasting fuel of the writer, free to savour the enchantment of being human among humans, unplagued as yet by having to worry in the first person about such issues as food and housing. But as long as the goat, tethered or not, manages to cut a few instructive capers on the way, I will be satisfied. What I write about fundamentally is not the tragedy of a stricken and contracting community but about fulfilment and its opposite, arrogance and the servility it feeds on, death and the dreams it puts an end to . . .

(THE BARRY HERALD, *4th July 1952*)

One of the two letterwriters in THE BARRY HERALD had said: *Mr. Thomas knows quite a lot about Spaniards and quite a lot about schoolboys. It is time we met some of these in his novels.* In two of his subsequent novels Gwyn was to fulfil these requests.

A FROST ON MY FROLIC (1953) is the author's only novel about school life and the only one about the Second World War; it is precisely set in the Spring of 1944. It is also the only one with a

36

teenage narrator, although this had earlier occurred in some of the stories (e.g. 'Simeon'). The
novel is really in two parts: the first six chapters
follow the progress of a school day, describing the
interrelation of masters and boys, firmly based in
the community of Mynydd Coch, which seems
to be a hybrid of the Rhondda and Barry.
Chapter 7, an interlude at the local cinema,
forms a coda, or it can be seen as an alternative
to chapter 6 in terms of the day's progression.
From chapter 8 to the end the scene is shifted
to a farming camp in the country, perhaps meant
to represent Dunraven, though there may also
be a recollection of the time the author spent in
Cardigan. The earlier chapters relate a series of
highly comic incidents, connected only by the
frame of the school day; chapter 6, on the school
firewatching activities, is Thomas humour in
classic form. There is also a rich crop of religious
sects: *the Marchers, the Drummers and the Lookers who
do even their shopping by scriptural injunction* (p. 10).
Tantalisingly, the Marchers are not defined, but
we have a rich account of the Lookers:

*These Lookers wait hourly for the Judgement and stand ready
to skip out of the road and work out a case in the comfort of
the ditch. They cannot be blamed for holding this view, for
life in Mynydd Coch has been bleak and confusing for a long
time past. With us you can take one of three roads. You can
wait for a job to begin or you can wait for the job to end or
you can do the thing in real style, say what the hell to man
and nature and wait for the universal blow-out. Having this
death-cell notion strong upon them the Lookers lay no great
stock on tidiness of appearance, this appearance standing a
good chance of being quite needless or even ridiculous a few
seconds after the last kiss of soap on skin, of run of comb*

*through hair. Ted has often been sent home by more sensitive
teachers who find that two or three smaller pupils can hide
behind Ted's mop and have a quiet day of it, and they give
him strict orders to have a trim even if he has to rub the top
two inches off against a wall. But back he comes untrimmed.
He always brings a note from his father, the Looker, saying:
'Leave it grow. I got my reasons. A Looker.' Either the
teacher thinks Ted's name is Looker and forgets to call him
Dolan, or, if he has heard of the sect, grows to believe that
Mr. Dolan is a trifling and partial Looker whose exclusive
object for looking must be hair.*

(A Frost on my Frolic, *pp. 17–18*)

The Drummers, as might be expected, are a much
noisier group:

*The Drummers are another sect in Mynydd Coch. They were
established by a very far-seeing young seer called Evan
Jacobs. Sitting disgruntled on the mountainside one night he
saw a cloud formation which resembled, he thought, a hand
cupped over an ear. This gives Evan the idea that God is
deaf. This idea squares well with the state of Mynydd Coch
which is nothing more than a quadrangle of slopes, coal, rent
and chaos. Walk through its streets and you get the impression
that no one is listening, that no one in this world has ever
listened. Our appeals, said Evan, are too quiet to be heard.
So he founds the Drummers and uses the collections to buy
drums. That was two years ago. The sect has grown. It is
surprising how many people enjoy drumming even when they
do not know what lies at the back of it. They enjoy it even
more when they feel that if they do it loudly enough it will
ease their sense of sin and lower the rent. Every time they
meet there is a scramble for the sticks.*

(A Frost on my Frolic, *p. 21*)

All Gwyn's writing of the early fifties is a glorious

celebration of the Rhondda he knew in his adolescence and early manhood, seen in a wonderfully golden glow. Even the more serious early novels and stories possess a strong heroic quality as they describe the downtrodden characters' attempts to fight back against the outsize forces that overwhelm them. In the comic novels, the unspeakably harsh economic reality of the thirties is consistently transmuted into a firm artistic creation and a white-hot optimistic vision. Paradoxically, when that vision begins to be matched against the reality of the fifties, when economic and social conditions had been much improved, the glow starts to fade, causing a diminution of the creative imagination and a partial disintegration of the style. This transition can be traced in THE STRANGER AT MY SIDE (1954). Here Edwin Pugh the Pang, a minor character in the earlier works, emerges as the protagonist. He falls under the influence of his brother-in-law, Theo Morgan the Monologue, an amoral opportunist, who *was a fierce enemy of dedicated earnestness in any shape or form, and . . . held a constant brief for the droll and satanic* (p. 11). Edwin Pugh determines to shake off his chapel morality and his lifelong enmeshment in the workers' struggles and is temporarily converted to 'brilliance, laughter, carnival': *'Let there be light'*, he says, *'and to hell with such paralysing thoughts as social security and international brotherhood'* (p. 58). The rest of the novel charts his uneasy and inconclusive attempts to find himself in *the whole squalid net of human relations spun by the deathless spiders of greed, absurdity and violence* (p. 64). He decides to find a cave *from which to express his contempt,* but there being none available he takes up residence instead in a doorless outside lavatory by the roadside, to the astonishment of the passers by: *Every time a bus passed he lifted his bowler and said that a little civility costs nothing* (p. 65).

Although THE STRANGER AT MY SIDE contains a brilliant succession of comic flashes, they are not sustained and elaborated as in the earlier novels. An enormous number of narrative motifs and new characters are introduced in rapid succession, piling upon one another and producing an effect of disintegration, which extends into the style:

Theo tried to interest some of the semi-mystical sects in the area in the value of Edwin as a handy symbol of the anti-rational impulses for which they took up the tongs but they all agreed that Edwin's move was too overt and gross for any sect that did not have plumbing as a theme in its curriculum. Then Theo hearing that some thinkers in the Western world, having renounced any strictly social solutions for the plagues of misery and weariness and taken a fruitless amble through the baroque chambers of the occult and the Oriental were now seeking specific drugs that would keep ecstasy and forgetfulness as accessibly handy as the groceries and enable the voters faced by any menacing doctrine or State to slip in the necessary pellet and ignore the whole thing. Consciousness, said Theo, is the only hub around which the absurdities of which evil is made can possibly crystallise, and our sexton Waldo Slee rattled the gates of the Black Meadow to second that notion officially. Theo put Uncle Edwin into contact with an experimental herbalist known as Caney the Cure and Caney delivered some leaves which Edwin was to take after boiling. He did so and was cracked about the house like a whip asking to be aimed at some part of the roof where there was a hole. This herb turned out to be some African simple

40

used on dromedaries that were sick of sand and loads.
(THE STRANGER AT MY SIDE, *p. 65*)

There can be no doubt that the author himself regarded this novel as a kind of watershed when, in 1971, he described it as

an attempt to write a philosophic novel that could serve simultaneously as a comic script. The effort was so knotting it left me in a permanent state of mental hernia. It hastened my drift away from fiction and towards the theatre and a state of discursive introspection.
(ARTISTS IN WALES, *pp. 71–72*)

Another comment in that same essay is of great interest; whereas in the BARRY HERALD letter of 1952 Gwyn had seen the writer's task as that of a miner, tunnelling for his material underground, nineteen years later he sees himself as the pit:

A writer digs mercilessly into himself. By the time he is done he is a honeycomb of bewilderments, hollow enough to be eternally his own sad drum. He wonders how the paths and tunnels ever came to be formed.
(ARTISTS IN WALES, *p. 74*)

The attempt to marry the earlier comic vision to the changed conditions of the fifties is more sustained in A POINT OF ORDER (1956). The change of narrative technique already begun in THE STRANGER AT MY SIDE, in which the 'I'-narrator is Edwin Pugh's nephew, takes a step further here in that the first-person narrator is the protagonist, Alderman Eryl Pym, a former revolutionary who finds himself under attack from young militants in his diluted role of moderate liberal and from the moral conformists as *a bolshevik wolf in liberal clothing* (p. 48). The alderman's success in five consecutive elections is a victory for cynical opportunism, and the novel is another expression of the author's savage disappointment at the rout of proletarian ideals in the postwar period. The novel provided the basis for a radio play, THE ALDERMAN, broadcast in 1966. Of the radio plays of the fifties, the funniest is VIVE L'OOMPA (1955), the story of the brass band from THE WORLD CANNOT HEAR YOU going on a trip to Paris. THE LONG RUN (1958) is a radio portrait of Guto Nyth Bran, the Welsh runner who covered legendary distances.

The fragmentation of the author's creative imagination during this period no doubt led him more to the radio play, where he achieved very great success, and to the short story, a form in which he had always been a consummate artist. The variety of the stories he published in PUNCH and other journals then and later is astonishing, ranging from a parody of Lloyd George's love letters in 'Blue Ribbons for a Black Epoch', the outline of a satirical play in 'The Pelt of the Celt that Bit Me' (which was later to be expanded into LOUD ORGANS), the quiet menace of the cat-stealing Miss Pringle in 'Good Night, Julius', to the hilariously practical Miss Sanders in 'Who That Up There?' (all these are reprinted in THE LUST LOBBY).

THE LOVE MAN (1958) is quite distinct in setting and subject-matter from all Gwyn's other works, and is the only one of his novels written in third-person narration. Loosely set in seventeenth-century Seville (certainly not in Toledo, as the publisher's blurb mistakenly claimed), it is based more on Tirso de Molina's moralistic play on Don Juan, *El burlador de Sevilla* ('The Mocker of Seville', written in the 1620s), than on José Zorrilla's romantic conception in his *Don Juan Tenorio* (1844), though Dr Marañón's psychological interpretation may have been more important than either of the plays. The theme is really that of the male menopause, which has come somewhat early to Don Juan at the age of 35, brought on by the excesses his public expects of him. Far from being dragged down to hell by the Stone Guest (a story put out for the birds), he is kept prisoner by his uncle the bishop in the Inquisition's dungeons in order to spare the family honour. After having the bishop poisoned, Governor Pacheco, the regional tyrant, forces Don Juan to become one of his gang of *espadachines* who bully and murder the local inhabitants. After Pacheco's death, Don Juan ends up under the thumb of a vengeful María Vidal, whom he had earlier spurned. This ironical destruction of the legend is superbly narrated. All the characters are unsympathetically presented, the most monstrous being the innkeeper and his wife, who have a long history of murdering their guests and burying them in an olive-grove. Despite the modernity of the dialogue, the basic savagery of seventeenth-century Spanish politics is well captured.

Although a number of Gwyn's novels were banned by the Irish Censorship Board, all of them had been separately published in the United

States up to and including THE WORLD CANNOT HEAR YOU and some of them had been translated into other languages. From 1952 none of them received separate American editions, no doubt because of the rise of McCarthyism there, as Pearl Zinober points out in her unpublished thesis on 'A Study of Aspects of Gwyn Thomas's Humor' (Iowa State University, 1970). This can be seen to be particularly ironic since it was precisely at that time that Gwyn was moving more towards straight comedy, though there could be found, no doubt, sufficient revolutionary side-swipes in the comic novels for them to be censured. Only THE LOVE MAN was considered safe for publication in New York.

III

After THE LOVE MAN Gwyn Thomas wrote no more novels; *'the novel is not dead'*, he told me, *'only the novelist'*. His very successful attempts at writing dialogue for the radio plays he wrote in the fifties led him along a natural course towards the living theatre. The problem was that, unlike the Anglo-Irish, the Welsh had no tradition of professional theatre of their own, though enthusiastic amateur groups flourished throughout Wales. The country had a long history of sending a steady supply of actors and actresses to London, some of whom became world-famous, and in the late thirties there had been isolated examples of Welsh dramatists having their work produced in London. In 1938 Jack Jones won a play-writing competition with his LAND OF MY FATHERS, which was well received at the Fortune Theatre in London; later that year the play was translated into Welsh and had an enthusiastic reception at the Prince of Wales Theatre in Cardiff at the time of the National Eisteddfod. His RHONDDA ROUNDABOUT ran for a few weeks at the Globe Theatre, London, in 1939. Also in 1938, Emlyn Williams's THE CORN IS GREEN opened in London and received great critical acclaim and popular success (he had had a similar success in 1935 with NIGHT MUST FALL). But before the establishment of the Welsh National Theatre Company, and later, the Welsh Drama Company, there had been no professional centre in Wales where a native dramatist could get his work performed; it was

London or nothing.

Gwyn prepared THE KEEP to meet this challenge, and nature conspired to give its opening a cold douche: its first private performance at the Royal Court Theatre on 7th August 1960 was abandoned because of a cloudburst which flooded the stalls. It was ecstatically received when it was performed a week later, and a revised public production was prepared for 1961, which had a long and successful run and won for the author the Daily Mail Drama Award. The critics were almost unanimous in praising its rich dialogue and verbal wit, which came as a pleasant surprise after the more turgid styles to which they had grown accustomed. They did not, however, dwell greatly on the theme. The play is a satire on the muffling effects of the family institution and describes the interplay of manipulator and manipulated within the cosy citadel, 'the keep'. This is the only work in which the author leaves the larger canvas of an enclosed society and limits himself to an enclosed family group, and it works well within the confines of a two-act play. THE KEEP is set in South Wales in 1954, and we sense through the humour the playwright's disillusion with Welsh post-war society, which was first noticeable in THE STRANGER AT MY SIDE. The fact that the South Welsh valleys of the twenties and thirties were an economic disaster area caused bitterness in the author, but one sees that he had hopes of a great proletarian cultural flowering; this idea is present in all the novels and stories of Gwyn's first period. In his middle period those hopes are seen to turn slowly into ashes, and the reason for this, ironically, is the comparative affluence of the post-war epoch. It is not seen so much to be the result of emigration from South Wales of its potential intellectual leaders; this had always occurred, and the post-war growth of the University of Wales had indeed helped to staunch the flow. It is attributed rather to an enclosed cosiness, a new parochialism which implies the abandonment of earlier radical ideals. This disillusion will reach its most savage expression in LOUD ORGANS. In THE KEEP we see rather the reasons for the decline expressed through the Morton family. The father is a reformed drunkard, anxious not to offend anybody or anything. Among the five sons, Russell is the failed intellectual and Wallace the disillusioned doctor; as the author puts it in his prologue, *They waver uncertainly between the idealism of the pioneers who hoisted them from the ranks of the morlocks and the genial banality and hedonism of the man who has put his mind out with the cat.* Oswald is a recessive: *As soon as he finds the ghost, he will promptly give it up.* Only Alvin, the tinplate worker, has some remnants of the old political ideals, but he compromises them in attempting to come to grips with the new technological society. The appropriately named Constantine, the cynical and ambitious local government official, is the monster who manipulates the whole family, while their sister Miriam and the portrait of Mam, whom they believe to have been the victim of an American train crash, watch sardonically over them. Great irony is derived from the use as a *Leitmotiv* of an old revivalist hymn, '*Flee as a Bird to your Fountain, Ye who are Weary of Sin*'.

The static quality of the play increases the feeling

of claustrophobia. The events that affect the action all take place off stage: there is, as it were, a missing central act where the action occurs, while the audience sees only the reaction of the characters.

JACKIE THE JUMPER (1963) is in a sense ALL THINGS BETRAY THEE transposed to the stage. The setting, 'Ferncleft', is once more Merthyr Tydfil during the riots of 1831. Jackie Rees, the eponymous protagonist, represents John Simon Adams (the Dic Penderyn figure of the novel), his uncle the Rev. Richie Rees here stands for Mr Bowen the hypocritical divine, and John Ironhead Luxton replaces Richard Penbury the ironmaster, possessing a similar secret romantic sympathy for the proletarian leader. The playwright himself defines the theme in his prologue:

I wanted a play that would paint the full face of sensuality, rebellion and revivalism. In South Wales these three phenomena have played second fiddle only to the Rugby Union which is a distillation of all three. I wanted a theme that would illustrate this curious see-saw of passivity and defiance in human life. Why some stir it up and others allow the scum of conformity and defeat to form into a mortal pall above their heads. The urge to exult and couple at odds with the compulsive wish to geld and part. Dionysus beating the living lights out of St Paul and the other way about.

(*in* PLAYS AND PLAYERS, *February 1963, p. 27*)

There are some basic differences of structure between novel and play. The harpist, who is narrator of the novel and there appears to represent the author himself, is removed and replaced by the play's audience, while the figure

48

of Jackie is imbued with the harpist's yearning for rustic freedom away from *the pox of smoke and toil* but also with *the fiercely flowering libido*. After he has persuaded the people to move to a Utopian valley in North Pembrokeshire—a trek that ends disastrously at Llanddarog—Jackie decides to reform himself, which means giving up the struggle and selling out to the enemy:

ALL: *Speak out for us, Jackie. Sing out for freedom, boy. (Jackie looks around most craftily.)*
JACKIE REES: *Oh! no, I'm not going to speak. I'm not going to sing. Tonight I saw something in the eye of that uncle of mine that really put the chill on me. We're not joking any more, are we? Death is very clearly on the agenda. And something must have happened to me in that last trip around the hills . . . At the last farmhouse I stayed at, the farmer's daughter and I hit it off. She promised to join me on my palliasse one night. She did not come to me. And the palliasse was wet from a week's rain and a most considerable leak in the roof.*
GEORGE CHISLETT: *Something detained her, Jackie. Her father found out or she read a pamphlet about honour or disease. No girl in her right senses would betray you, Jackie.*
JACKIE REES: *I've had rheumatism ever since. My legs are slower. No, she wasn't detained. She didn't forget. I went to look for her. I found her. She was sharing the palliasse of the ploughboy. He was fifteen years younger than I. And he had a dry palliasse.*
GEORGE CHISLETT: *You killed him?*
JACKIE REES: *No, no. I'm telling you. Flames have gone down inside me. I felt no anger, no shame. Just a bit more draught as I stood there in my shift in the attic . . .*
GEORGE CHISLETT: *You're hungry and thirsty, Jackie. Two days of drinking, talking, dancing, and you'll be the same old Jackie.*

JACKIE REES: *No. I'm going to make an offering to Mr. Luxton and the Reverend Richie Resurrection Rees. The idle, seditious goat becomes the dedicated gelded toiler. I shall make amends for every slight I've ever offered the men of wealth and the sectaries. I shall offer myself for employment at the foundries at dawn tomorrow morning. And when I've done my twelve-hour stint, with the filth of labour still upon me, I shall present myself to my reverend uncle and swear upon his fattest Bible that from now on to the grave I shall be the most icily celibate creature this side of a monastery.*

(JACKIE THE JUMPER, *Act 1*)

Jackie thus embodies the 'failed leader' theme, as well as that of the tired libertine already encountered in THE LOVE MAN. His failure allows the establishment to take over once again: the county sheriff arranges for his execution and his revivalist uncle wins over the hearts of the people. The final mood is much more pessimistic than in ALL THINGS BETRAY THEE:

LUXTON: *You'll be left alone, you know.*
JACKIE REES: *What's that?*
(*The last of the sound dies away.*)
LUXTON: *Did you know that? Did you know that the fall of evening might bring the fall of hope, that once they saw that little circus of vindication out there they might slink away and leave you alone?*
JACKIE REES: *Oh! yes, yes. I knew that. Whenever you lead people against any citadel that's been whacking them over the head, it's just a trial run. Wanting to know how the legs will feel when they start in a new direction. And remember they've been whacked. They don't see too far, too clearly. Their legs are twisted and their feet are fearful. They have been made to stand in postures that are less than human.*
LUXTON: *And you'll be left alone.*

50

JACKIE REES: *Why not? Other people tear your arms out. But they are nourished on the memory of the man they dismembered. All the way along the road, the unburied dead trying to explain and warn. I've made two mistakes, Mr. Luxton. One, never having looked hard enough for a woman who could dominate me, shape me, kill me.*
LUXTON: *And the second?*
JACKIE REES: *Having tried to interpret the dreams of people who didn't even know they were asleep.*
(JACKIE THE JUMPER, *Act 3, p. 294*)

The music which follows all the moods of the play is used with great ironic effect at the close: as the abandoned Jackie is led off to be hanged, a choir softly sings 'Hail to the Lord's Anointed', the same hymn that the crowd sang exultantly when they were still following Jackie at the end of Act 2. JACKIE THE JUMPER has a tremendous impact: full of movement of song and dance in the first act, it has a flatter second act, set in the Luxton mansion, but menaced by the imminent arrival of the rioters, and a third act set in a country inn, where Jackie's friends are found singing a Sunday School marching hymn, 'Awn ymlaen i'r fuddugoliaeth' *('Onward to victory')*, but this final act slowly fades into an elegiac mood for the doomed hero.

LOUD ORGANS (1962) is the most savagely satirical of Gwyn's plays. It is a musical in two acts set in Tiger Bay, Cardiff, during the affluent sixties. The scene comprises part of a waterfront street and the Cot Club and Bingo Hall constructed out of what was once a chapel. The chief character is the manipulator, Theophilus Wffie Morgan, a former boxing manager, now a wholesale fruit and vegetable merchant and pimp. He controls the other characters, in the same way as Con in THE KEEP. The manipulated consist of three club hostesses, three ex-boxers turned waiters, three rugby boys, and the headwaiter Nimrod Pym, an ex-minister who has been thrown out of his pulpit and whom Wffie Morgan has salvaged from meths-drinking. The ghost of a famous boxer who has escaped from Wffie Morgan's circus, Alfie the Mighty Atom, hangs over the proceedings (like Mam in THE KEEP). At the end it is revealed that, far from having been murdered by Nimrod Pym in an alcoholic blinder, he has taken refuge with The Quiet People, a religious community in Breconshire. A mysterious stranger, Jim Bumford, enters at the beginning of the play and disturbs Wffie's arrangements. Gradually it is made apparent that he is a failed Hollywood script-writer, who is hired by a chapel-minded London-Welsh tycoon to do an exposure of Morgan's nefarious activities in the converted chapel. This extraordinary fantasy is performed with a series of thumping songs and occasional balletic routines.

When the play was performed in Cardiff, some of the audience appeared to be shaken by the frank references to depravity and prostitution, but they may have been stung more by the satirical attacks on contemporary South Welsh society, as expressed, for example, in 'The Rugby Song':

> *Up and under, up and under,*
> *That's the thunder from the hills,*
> *Rugby outings are the answer*
> *To the dark Satanic mills.*

GWYN THOMAS

If you talk to us of grief and such,
We say grab the ball and kick for touch,
In the face of the trampling foe
Take a dive and tackle low.

Fugitives from thought are we,
Sons of heavy industry,
Satisfied artisans, labour's cream,
We've sold the pass on old dad's dream.
We've buried Hardie, banished Marx,
Give us hedonistic larks;
Car in garage, cash galore,
Was ever life like this before?

Better than a speech by Nye
Is the cry of Kelly's eye,
Kelly's eye, Kelly's eye,
Kelly knows, Kelly sees
We've won a wondrous social ease;
All thought vanquished, crises past,
We're on the gravy train at last.

Fish and Fish, to hell with chips,
Ten pints of best, twelve whisky nips.
Chicken suppers, trips to Spain,
No more conflict, park your brain.
For total peace inside your heads,
Take our cue and pot the Reds.
We've got everything we've ever prized
In a Britain semi-socialised.

One tenth cultured, semi-free,
Fugitives from thought are we.
Dialectic, cease to tease us,
Slumps will come no more to freeze us.

So three cheers now for the Iron Men
Who'll bring us glory once again
At Twickenham, at Twickenham.
Hearts of steel and skulls of teak,
Through them let modest Gwalia speak.
We may desert our ancient Muses
But let the Saxon count his bruises
At Twickenham, at Twickenham.

Up and under, up and under,
That's the thunder from the hills;
Rugby outings are the answer
To the now hygienic mills.

(LOUD ORGANS, *Act I*)

The parody of a bingo session, with Wffie Morgan
first calling the numbers and then the ex-
preacher Nimrod Pym, who causes a near-riot
among the players, is a classic Thomas scene:

WFFIE: *Arise, O Sun, Twenty-one. Weep no more, Forty-*
four. Earth's your heaven, Thirty-seven. Learn New Tricks,
Fifty-six. Cheat the State, Thirty-eight. Change your mate,
Thirty-eight. What's yours is mine, Fifty-nine.
VOICE: *House. House!*
WFFIE: *That's the lucky lady. Cashier, pay the lady.*
(*Wffie comes swinging out into the room. The rugby boys are*
behind him. They are looking a bit bemused as if this might
be the first time they have seen Bingo with perfectly clear
eyes.)
WYN: *They are very intent, very numb, Wffie. There are*
some of them in there, you could take a leg off and they
wouldn't notice.
WFFIE: *That's the game. Organised on a proper Babylonian*
scale by some sleepless genius like myself it could oust all such
nuisances as systematic thought, remorse and God knows what

54

else. King Bingo to the Queen of Carnal Delight. God, they sit so still with their little cards. (He turns to the boxers) Have you heard of Pavlov?

PANCHO: *Who did he manage?*

WILLIE: *He was a wrestler.*

WFFIE: *He was a wizard, a whip-master of the nerves. Every time he rang a bell the Government increased the dog licence . . .*

NIMROD: *Ration hate, Twenty-eight. Love in wine, Thirty-nine.*

Love's too late, Forty-eight.

Oh where's the road to Babylon? Thirty-one. Thirty-one!

Who'll bring Jezebel together again?

Three times ten; three times ten!

You'll meet more than one angel on the way back from heaven. Forty-seven, forty-seven.

When Sodom was burning, for excesses of glee

The gut of a whale was a shrewd place to be.

But Jonah the prophet, he entered a plea.

I know that it's safer, but what's here to see?

Fifty-three! Fifty-three!

(There is a pause and frenzied voices are heard.)

VOICES: *Go on. Go on!*

NIMROD *(very quietly): Who's alive?*

VOICES: *The number! Give us the number!*

NIMROD: *(raising his voice): Who's alive?*

VOICES: *The numbers, the numbers, the numbers, we've got no light without the numbers.*

NIMROD: *Then make fresh light, you crumby loons. Look at yourselves, you poor staring paralytics.*

(There is, but only for a moment, a terrible silence. Then there are noises that suggest a murderous rage among the bingo mob.)

VOICE OF PANCHO: *Buck up, Nimrod, boy. Don't upset them. (He addresses the players.) Keep calm now. Here's your gripe-water. Here's your talc. (The boxers go into a*

frenetic list of numbers and there is a great choral 'Oh!' of
relief as the players sink back into their velvet mental shroud.)
(LOUD ORGANS, *Act 2*)

All the characters have quiet moments when
they recall their innocence, lost in the distant
past; sometimes they express this in sung verse,
as in the duet sung by Nimrod Pym and Mollie,
one of the hostesses:

In the old dark park of remembrance
The paths are in circles and long
The stars and a touch of the fingers
Are all that can guide us along
To a place in the park where peace will grow
Where the dark has a pattern we seem to know
Where the trees won't tremble as they have long since
Where the mind falls silent and the nerves won't wince
For the past is a park in a haunted town
The past is a park that we walk in.
(LOUD ORGANS, *Act 1*)

The play attempts to capture the popular ethos
of South Wales in the 1960s, with the memory of
the dismal yet idealistic past haunting the false
gaiety and mindlessness of the present. Yet it is
not artistically successful; there are signs of a
running out of steam. The play lacks the shaping
principle and the sustained vitality of the earlier
works, as though the artist found himself as lost
as the society he was trying to satirise.

The dramatist's second musical play, SAP, com-
missioned by the Welsh Arts Council, was first
performed in Cardiff in 1974. It is set in the Great
War and is entirely surrealistic, as the opening

stage directions indicate:

(*The Great Arch beneath which War and Death crawl, over which life struts and sings, is lit only from beneath. We see the trench in which men wait frozenly. To the right of trench is a deeper level on which men burrow and sap . . . To the right, on eye level with men looking out from their position on the firesteps, is an eerily lit jungle of barbed wire. On furthest coil a man lies quite still. One of the men in trench, moved by rage and pity, stretches out his hand towards his dead comrade. A shell whines down and a grumbling roar of men mounts upward. When the two notes meet they explode into a great harmony. The stage is flooded with light and the soubrettes, flag-sellers, white-heather sellers, Tory squiresses, march over arch singing a rapturous version of the Welsh Sunday School rouser, with English lyric, 'Awn ymlaen i'r fuddugoliaeth', 'Forward to victory'. A bullet whizzes past the ear of the lad who has imprudently, with his outstretched hand, exposed himself to pity and a shattered head.*)*
1st Soldier: *Christ!*
2nd Soldier: *Where?*
3rd Soldier: *Missing without trace.*
(*The soldiers and sappers whistle an accompaniment to 'Forward to Victory'. The big lights dim and the music ceases. When the sappers and soldiers begin to speak their accents never move very far from the Taff and the Tawe.*)
(Sap, *Act 1*)

The sappers and soldiers in the trenches on the lowest level of the stage maintain an intermittent commentary throughout the action. On the middle level, the stage is filled alternately with a Welsh chapel with choir-filled pews, a recruiting meeting, a music-hall with soubrettes, and the ward of a military hospital with dancing nurses. On the apex of the arch which surmounts the

stage, there appear from time to time the generals
and politicians, the Mogul, the lecherous revivalist preacher and contraltos wearing patriotic
sashes. Through these scenes wanders the Poet,
pondering on the zany activity around him:

*(The stage darkens except for the spot that falls on the Poet.
There is an assembly humming of the Boer War song, 'Oh
break the news to mother'.)*
POET: *We have two gifts. One for the making of elegies.
The other for creating opportunities for its exercise. Deep
within all societies there is a childish distrust of human
purpose. When the night-wind strikes me these thoughts form
in my head-bones like a migraine. A damned good funeral is
still one of our best and cheapest acts of theatre. I am the
thought that will persist, the mind that won't lie down. I am
the prophet of a jagged recollection in the mind of the timid
sage and the raging clown. I shall stand behind the victors at
their feasts of tribal boasting. And in the minds of those
strange men who lead the nations into toils of pain, I shall
cause a thought or two to bleed until the truth of mercy once
again becomes a need. An idiot's creed, but it may breed.
I will maintain my watch here till the last curse has been
said. Between the little lusts of the living and the monstrous
peace of the dead. And that is me talking through a hole in
my head on behalf of the dead. I will project some sound of
love from the core of what I was and am. The world will bend
its head to hear. And the world won't give a damn.*

*(He turns his head and listens intently. Two sounds are
heard. One a men's chorus beginning softly and sardonically
to sing 'Be careful little hands'. The other is the roll of
the guns.)*

*The sounds of love. A stupid phrase but possibly seminal.
Oh, what a song we'd make if we could gather up all the
sounds of love that are wasted now in whispers.*

(The gunfire sounds recede. The singing mounts.)

(SAP, *Act I*)

The end of the first act coincides with the end of the first phase of the battle of the Somme Salient, with the generals quarrelling with the politicians over the reinforcements. The second and final act begins with the return of Willie John James, a Lloyd George figure, to South Wales where he faces a hostile crowd because he has forcibly ended a coal-strike:

WILLIE JOHN: . . . *Do you realise that when your leaders go out into the world they make a slight change of species? The heaven you sing of in your chapels is a big hotel. I've been there. It's fine. The first ape to become a partial man did so when he first wandered out of the woods on trade-union business, and bust a gut doing a Jesus job on the wounds of the working people. But not me. Not me. There are easier ways, easier ways. Mr. Matlock the Moloch found me a safe seat as a Christian collaborationist. The two great parties of velvet attitudes and flawless manners opened their doors to me. Away from the cottage smell, the proletarian snarl. Get the run of the syllables there. That was the sort of phrase that made me one of the golden hinges of the coalition currently guarding the grail of democratic decency. Lovely! I buried my pacifism and socialism in a grave so deep I struck coal and Mr. Matlock made a new pit out of it. Last night, in my old village, a woman spat at me and screamed, 'Willie John James, you have the deaths of thousands on your conscience. How can you stand it, Willie John James?' I wept in front of her to show my guilt. But the tears were quick to dry. I'm not vulnerable up here. I'm clear away from the flesh and passion of my beginnings. I will watch humanity bleed to death. Pity, pity. But each one to his own madness. I'll take pleasure in making memorable speeches about it. But no*

*woman will ever creep from behind my cradle and spit at me
again.*
   *(A great drumming to suggest some new eruption of the
offensive and the men sing the Salvation Army anthem, 'We
will meet a Friend when we cross the river' . . .)*
                                          (SAP, Act 2)

The remaining disastrous phases of the battle
pass, and as the last gunfire is heard, the
Boy, representing the innocent cannon-fodder, is
killed by a sniper's bullet. The ending of the play
is as sardonic in tone as the opening:

*(The Politician, Willie John James, dressed as he was when
he appeared at the beginning of the play, enters bearing a
great wreath of poppies.)*
THE POLITICIAN: *Time like an ever-rolling stream
                         Bears all its sons away.*
SERGEANT: *Hang on a bit with me.*
THE POLITICIAN: *They fly forgotten as a dream
                         Flies at the opening day.*
(He lays the wreath on the body of the Boy.)
CORPORAL: *They'll see to that.*
*(A great musical montage. A wave of schmaltz anthems,
hymns and ballads. They lead into 'Forward into victory'.)*
                                     (SAP, end of Act 2)

The entire performance is punctuated with
music. The rousing revivalist hymns are used
satirically: 'I'm H-A-P-P-Y I am', sung and
danced by nurses and one-legged soldiers; a ribald
rendering of 'When the roll is called up yonder
I'll be there'; an action performance of 'Tele-
phone to Glory, all joy divine, I feel the current
moving down the line'. At the play's première in
the Sherman Theatre, Cardiff, the public seemed

60

to accept the author's attempt to deflate false sentimentality in his satirisation of these hymns, but the mainly Welsh audience appeared to have more difficulty in accepting the incongruous settings for the more cherished Welsh hymns and songs:

(. . . *The mass-singing stops abruptly. A solitary voice is heard singing the old Welsh heart-stirrer 'Cartref'. A roaring voice asks:*)
1st Sapper: *How the hell did we got here? Are you listening, God? Are you looking this way, Lloyd George? Who put us here?*
(*Brilliant light. Across the arch comes a gay procession led by a Horatio Bottomley-like figure, a Bute Street Mogul, beating a big drum.*)

(Sap, *Act 1*)

Songs like 'Cartref' can normally be relied on to create a wave of cosy warmth, but from time to time throughout the play the author skilfully allows this mood to develop, only to deflate it ruthlessly. The only occasion on which he exempts the audience from these attacks on their sentimentality is in the final scene, just before the Boy is killed, when the Sunday-school hymn 'Just as I am, without one plea' leads into the last needless sacrifice:

Boy: *You've forgotten God.*
(*The others just lift their hands and stare at the Boy in a gentle astonishment.*)
Do you know what happened to me a year ago? In one week, in one week, the two eyes of my life went out. My father was killed in the pit, and Mr. Wilkins, my Sunday School teacher, was killed over here. Mr. Wilkins was a saint. He

*could explain sin and death. He could explain them a treat.
You could see sin and death limping up to apologise for being
such a nuisance to the hearts of men. At the end of that week
I was in the dark. I told myself that I would go to the chapel
and tell them that where my faith had been I was now holding
a bucket of ash, and I was going to pour it over them. I went
to the service. I left my place in the congregation and went
to stand on the pulpit steps. Mr. Billington, the precentor, the
man who led the singing, very loud, very vain, Mr. Billington,
he tried to push me away. But he must have felt something
cold inside me. His hand drew back. There was a great bank
of lilies in front of the pulpit. Through the lilies I saw a girl's
face. A pale face, smiling in a kind of sorrow. The windows
of the chapel were huge and bulging with light. The shadows
dropped away from me and I began to sing.
(He begins very slowly to sing the 'Just as I am' melody with
the words. He has a voice of great penetrating sweetness. The
drums play the same kind of accompaniment as before.)
Doesn't that prove something?*

CORPORAL: *It proves that you had a need to be standing on
steps singing.*

BOY: *It meant that I knew I had something to do on this
earth (he turns towards parapet and stands on firestep) that
I would have the power to stand up before those men out
there and . . .*

*(He stands on tip-toe, flings his arms towards the German
lines and is immediately toppled by a sniper's bullet . . .)*

(SAP, *Act 2*)

SAP contains the apotheosis of all the author's
preoccupations: the stained leader of the proletariat, the lecherous revivalist preacher, the
inhuman general, the commercial exploiter. The
themes of chapel morality, lechery and political
chicanery are cleverly combined in the Great War
setting through the figure reminiscent of Lloyd

George, who managed, incredibly, to embrace them all in his own *persona* while directing the course of the War. The Poet puts over the playwright's views, while the sappers in the trench act as a wry Greek chorus. It is a remarkable piece of writing, which had the splendid fortune in its first production to find an outstanding director in Michael Geliot, and an actor of genius in Keith Baxter, who played the three parts of poet, politician and evangelist with a deep understanding of the author's attitudes.

The author's latest play, THE BREAKERS (1976), is a Welshman's commemoration of the Bicentenary of the United States. The three acts take place in 1776, 1876 and 1976, respectively; the first two in Patience House, Tally, Pennsylvania, and the third in Pennsylvania House in Belford, South Wales. The theme of two centuries of dissent is explored through the fortunes of the Bowen family, whose members have emigrated from the Rhondda and are not finding life so very different:

DAN BOWEN: *By God, bailiffs and evictions over there in Wales. Indians and arrows over here in America. Wherever you are, somebody is waiting with bad news. (He peers out of window.) They've heard the guns. They're running away. Back there where we came from I spent most of my time running. Same thing here. Different things to run from. But running just the same. I wish I could stand still long enough to explain things to those Indians.*
MEG EVANS: *This will be a good year to see the end of. First that trouble with the chickens, then the blight on the potatoes, then this war against the King.*
DAN BOWEN: *No end to it. They take turns to go mad,*

chickens and men. I never thought I'd feel sorry for a King, but when I hear those smart alecks coming in here and blackening Britain's eyes and wanting to cut loose from the Crown, I feel like nipping back over the water, shaking that old George by the hand and telling him to stand firm . . .
(THE BREAKERS, *beginning of Act 1*)

Not only are the Bowens exploited by the local land agent, Aaron Tucker, they are also divided by the War of Independence in which one of the sons, John, is a captain in Washington's army, while his father and brothers support the Crown. The father, Dan Bowen, having embezzled funds belonging to the rebel army, refuses to take part in John's grandiose schemes to write the family's name on the banner of Independence, and, when Washington crosses the Delaware, makes good his escape on the next boat back to Wales. In the second act, the descendants of Dan Bowen, having emigrated from Trebanog to Avondale in 1868, are exploited workers of Sam Williams, an iron and coal master, who is alarmed by the activities of the Molly Maguires. Suspecting the Bowens of involvement in that movement, he attempts to buy them over to the side of management. They make their escape and return to Wales.

The third act shows the Bowens trapped in the prosperous Wales of the 1970s, with no possibility of emigration to America: *The lady on the statue has dowsed her torch and become truculent. Whatever dangerous gases were dispersed by the swirling mobility of yester-year will now be free to build up in the places of their origin* (author's programme note). The photograph of their late grandfather, Lord Alf Bowen,

64

a Labour life peer, looms over their opulent sitting-room and over them. Their father, Leroy Bowen, is a warned off bookmaker and pigeon-fancier *manqué*; the three sons are, respectively, a surgeon, a librarian and a television producer, and the two daughters a sociologist and a teacher of singing. Anthea the sociologist is the anti-heroine, a fanatical patriot whose politics feed on hatred:

ANTHEA BOWEN: *The filth of militarism will be the last thing we'll need. We shall wear a moral armour, no more. The brilliant phenomenon of the old vestry movement in a world that reeks of guilt. It's simple self-defence now. England has been the felon of the world. Now it's lurching, sick to death. It's blind, it gives no milk. Maggots from the imperial carcase come out waving phoney passports. Our disgrace was among the very first of her crimes. Let us at least avenge our crucified pride by turning our back in contempt on the old monster.*

(THE BREAKERS, *Act 3*)

Terrorised by her outbursts and frustrated by the emptiness of the society in which they live, her brothers and sister plan to emigrate to various parts of the globe, whence they will never return. The similarity of situation in this act to THE KEEP will be apparent, but this time they will depart in earnest, leaving a sobbing Anthea and her perplexed father on the empty stage:

LEROY BOWEN: *I don't know why but when they all went out there, for all the world like a little procession or demonstration, seen enough of those, too, reminded me of a song that my old dad, Lord Alfred Bowen, there, the good man who was possibly happy that he never had the chance to see*

*people kowtowing to him in his last dignity . . . There was
a song he grew fonder of as his life grew quieter. 'Absent' it
was called. 'Sometimes between long shadows on the grass,
The little truant waves of sunlight pass.' (He sings very
softly.) 'My eyes grow dim with tenderness awhile . . .'
(Anthea leans forward and utters one single, heart-broken
sob of exaggerated grief. Leroy looks expectantly at Anthea
but she says nothing.)
Truant waves, people are up to something, splitting up,
breaking away, spreading stains like a drunken outing. You're
right to be so down on drunken outings, Anth. No good at all.
Outings should never come back. Once, in a shop or a dream,
I don't remember which, I saw a great bowl of golden
light. Steady, golden light. I felt safe, as if all the kinds of
love I'd never been good at or lucky with would never again
put a foot wrong. Then a man rushed up and shouted,
'Save it. Save it'. The light went out. People are up to
something. That bloke was for a start. And I've had the
smell of dead magic about me ever since.
(The silence forms possessively around them again.)
You'll like the doves, Anth. They're Welsh, they tell me.
Toneless in their singing but Cymraeg to the core, I'm told.
(Anthea braces herself and looks around as if choosing the
bits of the universe she'll bother to pick up.)
Where's Australia, Anth? Where exactly is Australia?
(Anthea strides restlessly forth.)
What calls people? What do they hear that I don't hear?*
(THE BREAKERS, *end of Act 3*)

To a much greater extent than in THE KEEP, the
playwright sets the cultural and political vacuum
of modern Wales in a vast historical perspective:
emigration to America in the eighteenth and
nineteenth centuries is shown to have been an
abortive solution to the frustrations of the class
struggle at home. The political emasculation of

Wales in the post-war period is not seen to have found a positive solution in nationalism:

One member of the family is a prophet of national rebirth. The others stir uneasily within the old, normal reflexes of defeat and evasion. What way will the Welsh cat, which now regards being scalded as a hobby, jump this time? . . . Do the fragments of our old national experience cohere sufficiently to justify the image of a single animal? . . . Is there a new Philadelphia waiting within ourselves?
(author's programme note).

At the end of THE KEEP the characters wrap themselves up once more in their cosy cocoon; here they determine to break out of the trap.

As might have been forecast from the content of Act 3, the play's reception in Cardiff was mixed; unusually, perhaps, it caused difficulties within the Company before its première, not least because of its length and complexity. The one London critic who reviewed it, Mr Bernard Levin, accorded it very high praise:

It is a splendid piece of work; unhurried and profuse, but rich and sly, funny and content, inquisitive, virile, digressive and bright. In a word, alive, which is more than can be said for most of the plays I see in London, I can tell you. . . . the flesh is Mr Thomas's language, gleaming with his opaline wit. He writes as Shaw would have done if the etiolated Irishman had ever permitted himself brandy and good mutton; the very first words of the play jump like hot chestnuts . . . If I were in charge of the National Theatre . . . I would tip all that Austrian and Venetian rubbish into the Thames and import this product of the Marches.
(THE SUNDAY TIMES, 21st November 1976)

Despite various negotiations, it does not appear likely that this outstanding play will be seen in London in the near future; and the tragedy is that this is the prospect that faces any dramatist of promise in Wales today.

IV

Gwyn Thomas, more than most writers, has taken pains to explain what he has tried to do in his works, to clarify his attitudes to Welsh history and society, and to express his political attitudes. He has done this outstandingly well in his scintillating autobiography, A FEW SELECTED EXITS (1968), in a book of essays, A WELSH EYE (1964), and in a host of other essays and articles. During the sixties he appeared frequently on television discussion programmes, so frequently that he ran the risk of being taken for an instant pundit (he is fond of telling how the landlord of a mid-Wales tavern once mistook him for Dr Bronowski). He made some outstanding television series, including an important series of lectures on aspects of literature. Unusually, perhaps, for a creative artist, he is a sensitive and sharp-eyed critic of other writers' work. He therefore possesses the art of being the best critic of his own work: talking of SAP, for example, he wondered whether he could not have made his intentions clearer to the audience. The misunderstanding that has hurt him most was the charge that he had treated his prime materials—the people of the Rhondda—with derision or scorn. As Glyn Jones has so well put it: *to me it seems incredible that anyone could miss in Gwyn's work that great thundering note, that powerful underthrob of compassion that sounds throughout much of it. Surely Gwyn's humour at the expense of the poor and the underprivileged is uniformly genial and affectionate, never sardonic or wounding, never the sort to set a man apart from his community, to pillory him in his economic suffering, to deride him for his physical or social deficiencies* (THE DRAGON HAS TWO TONGUES, p. 121). Glyn Jones, however, considers that *Gwyn appears to have little sympathy with the national aspirations and the indigenous culture of our country* (*ibid.*, p. 122), and gives as an example his treatment of the chapels.

This criticism seems to me to stem from a mis-understanding of a number of the points Gwyn has tried to make: the historical decline in the use of the Welsh language, regrettable as that is, also means one less divisive factor in the socialist culture the author would have liked to see coming to fruition. The black side of the chapel culture lay in its muffling effects on the human spirit and its instillation of moral attitudes that led to political failure. These attitudes are seen to be incompatible with the ideal of a libertarian socialism. Gwyn is just as bold in his condemnation of nationalism: the ills it created historically are taken as a justification for condemning its rise in modern Wales as an absurdly anachronistic parochialism, at a time when internationalism is the order of the day. He fears, above all, that it will turn Wales into the cultural backwater of Europe. The author has every right to hold these opinions, and they should not cloud the task of literary judgement of his works.

He must be regarded as the supreme prose-poet of the Anglo-Welsh writers of the twentieth century, with an unsurpassed and original command of the riches of the English language, even among the English writers of his generation. He is certainly a humorist of great genius, possessing a mind, as Glyn Jones well describes it, *that enlarges and enlivens and decorates, which shoots up all its material as it were into massive and spectacular fountains, and plays upon them always the dazzling illumination of his wit* (THE DRAGON HAS TWO TONGUES, p. 123). He is also a moralist, of a very precious brand of morality, which at once unites him to those readers whose minds are on the same splendid beam as his own. In his writings for the theatre, he is pioneering a track for future Welsh dramatists in a stretch of country unexplored by earlier writers.

Gwyn Thomas's many and important contributions to Anglo-Welsh culture were recognised in 1976 by the presentation to him of the Honour, or Principal Prize, of the Welsh Arts Council. Despite this official recognition, it is probable that his work is more appreciated outside Wales than within it, and not only by Welsh exiles, as the size of foreign editions and the reviews published in various countries testify. This may be due in part to his views on the resurgence of nationalism, though these are probably shared by a majority of the working class in Wales. If the members of the new Welsh intelligentsia disregard his work on these grounds, theirs is the artistic loss. At least he has not deserted the place to which his mind abidingly returns.

Bibliography

GWYN THOMAS

I have tried to make this list as complete as possible, in view of the fact that no exhaustive bibliography has yet been published. The hardest task has been to track down the short stories and essays published or republished separately (the most important of these are here listed in a special section) and the dates of transmission of the radio and television plays (which are given when known).

Novels and Collections of Stories

WHERE DID I PUT MY PITY? *(Folktales from the Modern Welsh)*, London: Progress Publishing Co., 1946. 193 pp. (contains 'Oscar', 'Simeon', 'The Couch, My Friend, is Cold', 'Dust in the Lonely Wind', 'A Spoonful of Grief to Taste', 'Myself my Desert').

THE DARK PHILOSOPHERS, in TRIAD ONE, ed. Jack Aistrop, London: Dennis Dobson Ltd., 1946, pp. 81–193; Boston, Mass.: Little, Brown & Co., 1947. 178 pp.; reprinted in THE SKY OF OUR LIVES, London: Hutchinson, 1972, pp. 91–205; Boston, Mass.: Little, Brown & Co., 1972 *(novella)*.

THE ALONE TO THE ALONE, London and Brussels: Nicholson & Watson, 1947. 164 pp.;

American title: VENUS AND THE VOTERS, Boston, Mass.: Little, Brown & Co., 1948. 254 pp. *(novel)*.

ALL THINGS BETRAY THEE, London: Michael Joseph, 1949. 318 pp.; American title: LEAVES IN THE WIND, Boston, Mass.: Little, Brown & Co., 1949; reprinted New York: Monthly Review Press, 1968. 307 pp. *(novel)*.

THE WORLD CANNOT HEAR YOU *(A Comedy of Ancient Desires)*, London: Victor Gollancz Ltd., 1951. 288 pp.; Boston, Mass.: Little, Brown & Co., 1952 *(novel)*.

NOW LEAD US HOME, London: Victor Gollancz Ltd., 1952. 256 pp. *(novel)*.

A FROST ON MY FROLIC, London: Victor Gollancz Ltd., 1953. 285 pp. *(novel)*.

THE STRANGER AT MY SIDE, London: Victor Gollancz Ltd., 1954. 255 pp. *(novel)*.

A POINT OF ORDER, London: Victor Gollancz Ltd., 1956. 224 pp. *(novel)*.

GAZOOKA AND OTHER STORIES, London: Victor Gollancz Ltd., 1957. 200 pp. *(for 'Gazooka', see also Radio Plays; twelve other short stories)*.

THE LOVE MAN, London: Victor Gollancz Ltd., 1958. 221 pp.; American title: A WOLF AT DUSK, New York: Macmillan, 1959 *(novel)*.

RING DELIRIUM 123, London: Victor Gollancz Ltd., 1960. 192 pp. *(short stories).*

THE LUST LOBBY, London: Hutchinson, 1971. 223 pp. *(twenty-nine short stories).*

THE SKY OF OUR LIVES *(Three Novellas),* London: Hutchinson, 1972. 252 pp., and Boston, Mass.: Little, Brown & Co., 1972; reprinted London: Quartet Books, 1973. 215 pp. *(reprint of* THE DARK PHILOSOPHERS, *and of 'Oscar' and 'Simeon' from* WHERE DID I PUT MY PITY?*).*

Radio Plays and Feature Programmes

THE ORPHEANS, produced by Elwyn Evans, BBC Welsh Home Service, 2nd September 1952 *(60-minute play).*

GAZOOKA *(A Rhondda Reminiscence),* produced by Elwyn Evans, BBC Welsh Home Service, 11th January 1952; new production by Elwyn Evans, with the author in the role of Milton Nicholas, BBC Third Programme, 2nd January 1953, repeated 12th January and 9th October 1963 *(60-minute feature).*

FORENOON, produced by Denis Mitchell, BBC North of England Home Service, 25th January 1953 *(45-minute feature).*

FESTIVAL, BBC Welsh Home Service, 9th April 1953 *(60-minute feature).*

OUR OUTINGS, produced by Elwyn Evans, BBC

Welsh Home Service, 27th October 1953 *(60-minute feature)*.

THE DEEP SWEET ROOTS, produced by Denis Mitchell, BBC Home Service, 12th November 1953 *(play)*.

THE SINGERS OF MEADOW PROSPECT *(new version of* THE ORPHEANS*)*, BBC Welsh Home Service, 9th April 1954 *(60-minute play)*.

VIVE L'OOMPA *(The Story of a Welsh Brass Band that went to Paris)*, produced by Peter Duval-Smith, BBC Third Programme, August 1955 *(play)*.

UP THE HANDLING CODE, produced by Elwyn Evans, BBC Welsh Home Service, 15th November 1955 *(60-minute play)*.

TO THIS ONE PLACE, BBC Welsh Home Service, 26th November 1956 *(60-minute play)*.

MERLIN'S BROW, BBC Welsh Home Service, 18th October 1957 *(45-minute play)*.

THE LONG RUN, BBC Welsh Home Service, 17th July 1958 *(30-minute feature)*.

NOISE, 1960.

THE WALK OUT, produced by Elwyn Evans, BBC Third Programme, 7th March 1963 *(play)*.

THE ENTRANCE, produced by John Griffiths, BBC Light Programme, 29th April 1964 *(60-minute play)*.

THE ALDERMAN, produced by Herbert Davies, BBC Home Service, 17th January 1966 *(60-minute play)*.

THE GIVING TIME, produced by Lorraine Davies, BBC Radio 4, 19th December 1968 *(60-minute play)*.

HE KNOWS, HE KNOWS, produced by Lorraine Davies, BBC Radio 4, 3rd August 1972 *(45-minute play)*.

THE WORRIERS, produced by Lorraine Davies, BBC Radio 4, 22nd August 1974 *(45-minute play)*.

Television Plays

THE ORPHEANS.

THE SLIP, produced by Gilchrist Calder, BBC Television Service, 14th October 1962.

THE DIG, 1963.

THE KEEP *(adaptation of the theatre play)*, directed by David J. Thomas, BBC Television Service, 6th May 1964.

UP AND UNDER, March 1973.

Television Series and Major Programmes

WALES AND THE WEST, with John Betjeman, a series of six weekly programmes transmitted by

TWW Ltd. from 27th August 1962.

THIS WORLD OF WALES, with Richard Burton and Gwyn Thomas, transmitted by TWW Ltd. on St David's Day 1963 on all British ITV network; re-transmitted on the Ed Sullivan Show in the U.S.A. and on Canadian Television.

GWYN THOMAS LECTURES: THE WRITER AND THE WORLD, a series transmitted by Harlech Television Ltd. from 2nd January to 7th April 1968.

ONE PAIR OF EYES: IT'S A SAD BUT BEAUTI-FUL JOKE, directed by Gilchrist Calder, BBC 2, 6th September 1969.

Theatre Plays

THE KEEP, performed by The English Stage Company, directed by Graham Crowden, Royal Court Theatre, London, one private perform-ance, 14th August 1960; new production directed by John Dexter in same theatre from 22nd Nov-ember 1961; published London: Elek Books Ltd., 1962. 116 pp.

JACKIE THE JUMPER, performed by The English Stage Company, directed by John Dexter, Royal Court Theatre, London, 1st February 1963; published in PLAYS AND PLAYERS, February 1963, pp. 26–44, and in PLAYS OF THE YEAR, ed. J. C. Trewin, vol. 26 (1962–63), London: Elek Books Ltd., 1963, pp. 209–97.

LOUD ORGANS *(A Play with Music)*, presented by Richard Rhys, with music by Patrick Gowers and choreography by John Broom, performed in Grand Theatre, Blackpool, 22nd October 1962; New Theatre, Cardiff, 29th October 1962 *(unpublished)*.

THE LOOT *(a play for sixthformers)*, in *Eight Plays: Book 2*, ed. Malcolm Stuart Fellows, London: Cassell & Co., 1965.

SAP, performed by The Welsh Drama Company, directed by Michael Geliot, Sherman Theatre, Cardiff, 12th November 1974 *(unpublished)*.

THE BREAKERS, performed by The Welsh Drama Company, directed by Michael Geliot, Sherman Theatre, Cardiff, 16th November 1976 *(unpublished)*.

Essays and Autobiography

A WELSH EYE, London: Hutchinson, 1964. 176 pp.; Brattleboro, Vermont: Greene Press, 1965 *(eleven essays, with drawings by John Dd. Evans)*.

A HATFUL OF HUMOURS, London: Schoolmaster Publishing Co., n.d. [1965]. 163 pp. *(twenty-six essays)*.

A FEW SELECTED EXITS, London: Hutchinson, 1968. 212 pp.; American sub-title: *An Autobiography of Sorts,* Boston, Mass. and Toronto: Little, Brown & Co., 1968. 239 pp.

Autobiographical essay in ARTISTS IN WALES, ed. Meic Stephens, Llandysul: Gwasg Gomer, 1971, pp. 67–80.

Short Stories and Essays published separately (select list)

'The Hands of Chris', in SATURDAY SAGA AND OTHER STORIES, London: Progress Publishing Co., 1946, pp. 74–78.

'The Pot of Gold at Fear's End', in MODERN READING, no. 15 (May 1947), pp. 98–107.

'The Limp in my Longing', in MODERN READING, no. 16 (November 1947), pp. 131–38.

'Then came we singing', specially written for COAL; read on BBC Welsh Home Service in 1953.

'And a Spoonful of Grief to Taste' and 'Thy Need', in WELSH SHORT STORIES, selected by Gwyn Jones, London: Oxford University Press, 1956, pp. 266–79 and 279–307.

'I Think, Therefore I am Thinking', in THE ANGLO-WELSH REVIEW, vol. 10, no. 25 (1959), pp. 19–21.

Essay on 'Education', in THE NEW BOOK OF SNOBS, by various hands, London: Museum Press Ltd., 1959, pp. 131–40.

'The Seeding Twenties', in PICK OF TODAY'S SHORT STORIES, 13, ed. John Pudney, London: Putnam & Co. Ltd., 1962, pp. 186–93.

'Some inns in Wales', in Pub. A Celebration, ed. Angus McGill, London: Longmans, 1969, pp. 161–87.

'Arrayed Like One of These', in The Shining Pyramid and other Stories by Welsh Authors, ed. Sam Adams and Roland Mathias, Llandysul: Gwasg Gomer, 1970, pp. 111–21.

'O Brother Man', in Twenty-Five Welsh Short Stories, selected by Gwyn Jones and Islwyn Ffowc Elis, London: Oxford University Press, 1971, pp. 43–53.

'The Very Perishable Vision—or Culture went thataway', in Wheeler's Review, vol. XVII, no. 1 (late Spring 1971), pp. 22–25.

Criticism on Gwyn Thomas

Howard Fast, Literature and Reality, New York: International Publishers Co. Inc., 1950, chs. 13–15, pp. 67–77.

Glyn Jones, The Dragon Has Two Tongues, London: J. M. Dent & Sons Ltd., 1968, pp. 107–23.

Pearl Zinober, 'A Study of Gwyn Thomas's Humor', M.A. Thesis, Iowa State University of Science and Technology, Ames, Iowa, 1970 *(unpublished)*.

Acknowledgements

My greatest debt is to Gwyn and Lyn Thomas, my friends for many years, who gave me access to all the materials I needed. Lyn Thomas also helped me to track down the rarer bibliographical items. I am also indebted to Walter and Nest Thomas, who assisted me with the biographical detail and commented on the first draft of this essay. I received, too, valuable advice from my colleague Professor A. J. Smith and from the reader of the University of Wales Press.

Mrs Lorraine Davies of BBC Wales most kindly assisted me with details of the radio plays.

The Author

Ian David Lewis Michael was born in Neath, Glamorgan, in 1936. He was educated at Neath Grammar School, where he was taught French by Gwyn Thomas's elder brother Walter, and later at King's College, London, where he took his B.A. with First Class Honours in Spanish. He lectured in Spanish philology and medieval literature at the University of Manchester from 1957 to 1970, and gained his Ph.D. there in 1967. Since 1971 he has been Professor of Spanish at the University of Southampton.

His publications have been mainly on Alexander the Great in medieval Spanish literature (Manchester University Press, 1970, and 'Alexander's Flying Machine', Southampton, 1975) and on El Cid (THE POEM OF THE CID, Manchester and New York, 1975, Spanish edition, Madrid, 1976). He is now working on sixteenth-century romances of chivalry. The Leverhulme Trust has appointed him Faculty Fellow in European Studies for 1977–78 to undertake research in the Royal Palace Library, Madrid, and other Spanish archives.

This Edition,
designed by Jeff Clements,
is set in Monotype Spectrum 12 Didot on 13 point
and printed on Basingwerk Parchment by
Qualitex Printing Limited, Cardiff

It is limited to 1000 copies of which this is

Copy No. 932

ISBN 0 7083 0652 7